CALVIN'S INSTITUTES
A NEW COMPEND

BOOKS BY HUGH T. KERR

Calvin's Institutes: A New Compend

*A Compend of the Institutes
of the Christian Religion by John Calvin*

A Compend of Luther's Theology

Positive Protestantism

CALVIN'S INSTITUTES

A NEW COMPEND

Hugh T. Kerr, editor

Westminster/John Knox Press
Louisville, Kentucky

Selections are reprinted from *Calvin: Institutes of the Christian Religion,* edited by John T. McNeill and translated by Ford Lewis Battles (Volumes XX and XXI: The Library of Christian Classics). Copyright © MCMLX W. L. Jenkins. Used by permission of Westminster/John Knox Press.

First edition

Published by Westminster/John Knox Press
Louisville, Kentucky

PRINTED IN THE UNITED STATES OF AMERICA

9 8 7 6 5 4 3 2 1

Library of Congress Cataloging-in-Publication Data

Calvin, Jean, 1509–1564.
  [Institutio Christianae religionis. English]
  Calvin's Institutes : a new compend / Hugh T. Kerr, editor. — 1st ed.
      p.   cm.
  ISBN 0-664-25080-7

  1. Theology, Doctrinal—Early works to 1800. 2. Reformed Church—Doctrines—Early works to 1800. I. Kerr, Hugh T. (Hugh Thomson), 1909–   . II. Title.
BX9420.I65 1989
230′.42—dc20   89-32573

CONTENTS

BOOK TWO

SIN AND JESUS CHRIST THE REDEEMER

BOOK THREE

THE HOLY SPIRIT

BOOK FOUR

THE HOLY CATHOLIC CHURCH

FOREWORD

John Calvin was born in 1509 at Noyon, France, a cathedral town midway between the two more celebrated cathedral towns of Amiens and Reims. His father sent him to the University of Paris to study for the priesthood and then to Orléans to study law. But the son was not to be ordained into the Roman Catholic Church, though he became the outstanding church leader, next to Luther, in the Protestant Reformation. Nor was he ever to practice the legal profession, though he helped to rewrite the civil laws of the city of Geneva, and the Protestant tradition he founded has always been deeply involved in political and social as well as religious and theological matters.

John Calvin was not one to be emotional about his own religious experience. He tells us almost nothing of his early spiritual pilgrimage. On his deathbed, he sighed, "I am a wretched sinner," and he was buried in an unmarked grave. He does mention "a sudden conversion" when he was twenty-five years old, a conversion not so much like that of the apostle Paul or Augustine as a turning away from medieval Catholicism to the evangelical Reformation views that had already begun to circulate from Luther's Germany throughout central Europe and into Great Britain.

Two years later (1536), he published the first edition of the *Institutes of the Christian Religion*, which as textbook and theological system had a formative influence on the whole development of Reformed (as distinct from Lutheran) Protestantism. Going through several revisions and editions, the *Institutes* has been translated into many languages, and there will doubtless be more to come. Between the first edition (1536) and the last (1559), Calvin was also publishing tracts and essays of all kinds and writing commentaries on nearly every book of the Bible. All this time he was preaching constantly, and he was carrying on an extensive correspondence with everyone of any importance in the church and in public life and with countless lesser-known persons in need of sympathy or religious instruction.

Calvin's personality has always been a lively subject for debate. Calvin the theologian, the scholar, the preacher, the church leader was also a human being—though his detractors have questioned even that. His critics have accused him of being overly stern and severe, headstrong and stubborn, intolerant and cheerless. Whether Calvin is the sort of person to elicit friendly affection or not—and there has always been division of opinion on this point—his was a mind entirely bent toward the truth as he saw it. His utter devotion of intellect and commitment of heart to God and the divine purpose in Christ have always won the respect they deserve.

Unfortunately Calvin's name and theology have been unfavorably linked in the popular mind with two easily misunderstood doctrines: the sovereignty of God and election, or predestination. Certainly he had much to say about both; perhaps his fault was to say too much. It was not in his nature to be evasive with heretics, recalcitrant citizens, or difficult and divisive doctrines. He was convinced from the scriptures that God is sovereign in the process of salvation, that it is God in Christ who takes the initiative in our redemption, and that we have nothing whatever within us or about us deserving of the divine favor. For Calvin to speak of the sovereignty of God was not to add still another transcendental attribute to the classical definitions of deity but simply to put first things first in the order of the gospel.

The one thing that overwhelmed Calvin about Christian faith was the good news of God's redemptive approach to sinful humanity in Jesus Christ. It was because he was so sure of this that he could talk about total depravity, of our inability to save ourselves, and of God's justification of the sinner through faith in Christ. Calvin was no misanthrope; his concern was not to belittle humanity but to glorify God.

Election and predestination, it is important to note, do not figure in the structure of Calvin's *Institutes* until the end of Book III: that is, at the conclusion of the major doctrinal section of the work. Here the discussion arises as a theological consequence or implication of the sovereignty of God. Calvin's doctrine of election is simply his interpretation of how God seems to operate in the realization of a divine redemptive purpose. Calvin was not the first to introduce this controversial doctrine, though he went farther than either Paul or Augustine, both of whom he claimed as predecessors for his view. Whatever we may make of the doctrine (for good or ill, it seems distinctly uncongenial to the modern mind), for Calvin it had no melancholy fatalistic flavor but was a source of joy, assurance, and hope. In the midst of staggering odds, when it was an open question whether the Genevan Reformation would succeed or be smothered, Calvin and his colleagues found strength and took courage in the realization that it is God alone who saves, that there is a divine purpose in Christ which sinful humanity cannot thwart, and that, come good or evil, "the Lord God omnipotent reigneth."

A look at the various editions of the *Institutes* indicates that Calvin experimented with different kinds of structures for his theology. The first edition of 1536 was a small book of six chapters. The first three comprised the theological nucleus of the work, dealing with the Ten Commandments, the Apostles' Creed, and the Lord's Prayer. This threefold format had already been used by Luther in the arrangement of his *Small Catechism* (1529). Before that it had been used by Thomas Aquinas in his *Compendium of Theology* (1273). Indeed, this particular structural method goes back to Augustine's *Enchiridion* (421), often called by its subtitle, "Of Faith [Apostles' Creed], Hope [Lord's Prayer], and Love [Ten Commandments]."

By the time of the final, definitive edition of the *Institutes* (1559), the work had grown from a small to a very large book, and from six to eighty chapters. The organizing principle for this edition was simply the Apostles' Creed, and as it contains four major articles—God, Christ, Holy Spirit, Church—so Calvin divided the work into four corresponding books. He regarded this structure as especially adequate for the purpose of doctrinal instruction.

"Instruction" might be a more meaningful translation of the Latin *institutio* in Calvin's title. Instead of *Institutes of the Christian Religion,* we could read *Instruction in the Christian Religion.* Calvin tells us in the Preface to the 1559 edition that his purpose was "to prepare and instruct candidates in sacred theology for the reading of the divine Word, in order that they may be able both to have easy access to it and to advance in it without stumbling."

The continuing influence of Calvin's *Institutes* upon later theologians and thinkers is incalculable. Though many of his harsher doctrines have been softened, his comprehensive structure of Christian truth has always made its own appeal. Karl Barth, for example, in the first volume of his *Church Dogmatics,* notes approvingly that Calvin's method of interweaving biblical with doctrinal interpretation in the *Institutes* rightly recognizes the church's perennial responsibility to proclaim the word of God for each new day and age (I/1, pp.

16–17). Paul Tillich, who might not be expected to find John Calvin theologically congenial, observes that the dialectic between the knowledge of God and the knowledge of ourselves with which the *Institutes* begins "expresses the essence of the method of correlation" that is so central for Tillich's own theology (*Systematic Theology*, I, p. 63).

The fact is, however, that much of Calvin's system as well as much of his polemic against Roman Catholicism have become outdated and irrelevant for modern thought. Systems as such are under general suspicion in almost every area of life. Both sectarian apologetics and abusive anathemas against other traditions are disallowed in our more ecumenical and pluralistic situation. For example, the reform program initiated in the Roman Catholic Church by Pope John XXIII and Vatican Council II represents a radically different situation as between Catholicism and Protestantism and one that Calvin could not have anticipated.

It would be a pity if Calvin's positive biblical and theological views were ignored simply because they are often entwined with obsolete arguments and belligerent polemics. Beyond this, the sheer massive bulk of Calvin's 1559 *Institutes* can be for many overpowering and intimidating. These are some of the reasons for preparing a Compend. The idea is not new. Only twelve years after Calvin's death (1564), there appeared the first in a long list of digests.

This Compend, first issued in 1939 when there was nothing like it in the field, is now presented in a revised edition in the hope that it will help to fulfill the contemporary demand of students and others for authentic texts in the original sources of our religious and cultural tradition. The Compend follows the main development of Calvin's theology without lingering over his prolonged attacks on the Roman Church or on matters of only dated importance. The material omitted will be chiefly of interest to Calvin specialists, whereas what is included, though only a tenth of the uncut edition, accentuates Calvin's positive convictions as well as the doctrinal symmetry of the work as a whole.

Calvin's table of contents and his chapter headings have been replaced for this edition with a simpler, more analytical division, but the sequence of his argument has been maintained throughout. References to the original text are supplied, for purposes of verification and further study, in the margins of the Compend in three figures—II.iii.4, for example—denoting book, chapter, and section of the 1559 edition of the *Institutes*.

When the first edition of the Compend was published in

1939, John Allen's English translation was used for the selections. Allen's serviceable but rather stiff text first appeared in 1813, was frequently reprinted, and in America became the standard Calvin text, issued by The Westminster Press.

In more recent years, and in connection with the editing and publishing of the Library of Christian Classics, a new, highly acclaimed English translation of the *Institutes* was included as volumes XX and XXI of the Library. This new translation, under the editorial supervision of John T. McNeill, was prepared by Ford Lewis Battles (*Calvin: Institutes of the Christian Religion,* 2 vols., Westminster Press, 1960, 1734 pp.).

The Battles translation, together with an exhaustive footnote apparatus, extensive bibliographies, and seven indexes, clearly supersedes the older Allen text and, at the same time, provides a comprehensive and functional Calvin library in its own right. It is this Battles translation of the *Institutes,* with the permission and encouragement of Westminster/John Knox Press, that has been used in the selections for this revised edition of the Compend.

In his introductory comment about the many digests and abridgments of the *Institutes* over the years, Ford Lewis Battles said of the first edition of the Compend that it "consists of thoughtfully chosen selections." It now has the added merit of a more readable English translation, thanks to Battles' own prodigious and scholarly contribution. Since the Compend is designed for those who wish an introductory overview of the *Institutes,* Battles' elaborate system of superscripts and interpretive footnotes has not been duplicated here. But note that the letter *p* following a bracketed Scripture reference indicates a paraphrase, however slight. Also note: Vg. = Vulgate, the Latin translation of Scripture. Comm. = Calvin's Commentaries. Ellipsis points have been used to indicate the omission of material within a selection but not after it.

Literature on and about Calvin continues at a steady pace and gives evidence of the enduring importance of the Genevan Reformer. Battles' bibliography of Calvin literature up to 1960 covers twenty-seven pages. In her specialized study on *Women, Freedom, and Calvin* (Westminster Press, 1985), Jane Dempsey Douglass devotes twenty pages to annotated references and nine pages to a select bibliography. In the popular biography by William J. Bouwsma, *John Calvin: A Sixteenth-Century Portrait* (Oxford University Press, 1988), there are fifty-eight pages of notes and eight pages of updated bibliography. Bouwsma in his acknowledgments expresses his indebtedness to the Meeter Center for Calvin Studies at Calvin College, Grand Rapids. An International Congress for Calvin Research has been established in Münster, Germany, and Calvin seminars have met in such diverse places as Montreal and South Africa. All this and more indicates the continuing and growing interest in both specialized and general Calvin studies.

A major problem of contemporary linguistic concern, which was no problem at all in previous generations, relates to the current general use of inclusive language and the conflict this raises with the literary texts of yesterday. Calvin's language, whether in French, Latin, or English translation, was thoroughly masculinist. Jane Dempsey Douglass notes in the Preface to her book: "A modern reader will notice the masculinity of Calvin's language both about God and about people. . . . In a discussion of historical theology there seems to be no good reason to obscure this fact by modernizing the language. . . . Though it was tempting to try to make the translation 'inclusive' in the modern sense, since existing translations of the Latin obscure the distinction completely, the resulting style proved too 'feminist' for Calvin. I concluded that such an attempt would merely obscure the realities of the thought world of the sixteenth century" (pp. 8–9).

The Battles translation was prepared some years before the later imperative for inclusive language, but it is probable that the translator would have agreed with Douglass that we cannot make Calvin to be other than what he was in his own time.

A Compend, to be sure, cannot take the place of the original, and serious students of Calvin will know that for a complete understanding of the *Institutes* the unabridged editions and specialized studies must be consulted. If the Compend succeeds in directing some to the original, that would be warrant enough for its appearance; if it serves to introduce others to the great evangelical doctrines of the Reformation, that would be even more desirable.

That a compendium of this sort meets a need as a textbook or as supplementary reading in seminaries and divinity schools, as well as in religious studies departments of colleges and universities, is attested by the continuous publication of the Compend over a period of fifty years. The revised edition has been greatly improved at a number of points, and the newer Battles translation happily rescues Calvin from the charge that his literary style borders on the obscure.

The hope that the Compend will make Calvin better known prompts this new edition. In the vivid phrase of Philip Schaff, the American church historian of a former generation, "the Reformation was a deeper plunge into the meaning of the Gospel." This Compend is an invitation, and perhaps a springboard, to make that plunge in our day.

BOOK ONE
GOD THE CREATOR

I

THE KNOWLEDGE
OF GOD

1. THE KNOWLEDGE OF GOD
AND THE KNOWLEDGE OF OURSELVES

I.i.1   Nearly all the wisdom we possess, that is to say, true
and sound wisdom, consists of two parts: the knowledge of God and of ourselves. But, while joined by many bonds,
which one precedes and brings forth the other is not easy to
discern. In the first place, no one can look upon himself without immediately turning his thoughts to the contemplation of
God, in whom he "lives and moves" [Acts 17:28]. For, quite
clearly, the mighty gifts with which we are endowed are
hardly from ourselves; indeed, our very being is nothing but
subsistence in the one God.

Then, by these benefits shed like dew from heaven upon us,
we are led as by rivulets to the spring itself. Indeed, our very
poverty better discloses the infinitude of benefits reposing in
God. The miserable ruin, into which the rebellion of the first
man cast us, especially compels us to look upward. Thus, not
only will we, in fasting and hungering, seek thence what we
lack; but, in being aroused by fear, we shall learn humility. For,
as a veritable world of miseries is to be found in mankind, and
we are thereby despoiled of divine raiment, our shameful
nakedness exposes a teeming horde of infamies. Each of us
must, then, be so stung by the consciousness of his own unhap-
piness as to attain at least some knowledge of God. Thus, from
the feeling of our own ignorance, vanity, poverty, infirmity,
and—what is more—depravity and corruption, we recognize
that the true light of wisdom, sound virtue, full abundance of
every good, and purity of righteousness rest in the Lord alone.
To this extent we are prompted by our own ills to contemplate
the good things of God; and we cannot seriously aspire to him

before we begin to become displeased with ourselves. For what man in all the world would not gladly remain as he is—what man does not remain as he is—so long as he does not know himself, that is, while content with his own gifts, and either ignorant or unmindful of his own misery? Accordingly, the knowledge of ourselves not only arouses us to seek God, but also, as it were, leads us by the hand to find him.

I.i.2   Again, it is certain that man never achieves a clear knowledge of himself unless he has first looked upon God's face, and then descends from contemplating him to scrutinize himself. For we always seem to ourselves righteous and upright and wise and holy—this pride is innate in all of us—unless by clear proofs we stand convinced of our own unrighteousness, foulness, folly, and impurity. Moreover, we are not thus convinced if we look merely to ourselves and not also to the Lord, who is the sole standard by which this judgment must be measured. For, because all of us are inclined by nature to hypocrisy, a kind of empty image of righteousness in place of righteousness itself abundantly satisfies us. And because nothing appears within or around us that has not been contaminated by great immorality, what is a little less vile pleases us as a thing most pure—so long as we confine our minds within the limits of human corruption. Just so, an eye to which nothing is shown but black objects judges something dirty white or even rather darkly mottled to be whiteness itself. Indeed, we can discern still more clearly from the bodily senses how much we are deluded in estimating the powers of the soul. For if in broad daylight we either look down upon the ground or survey whatever meets our view round about, we seem to ourselves endowed with the strongest and keenest sight; yet when we look up to the sun and gaze straight at it, that power of sight which was particularly strong on earth is at once blunted and confused by a great brilliance, and thus we are compelled to admit that our keenness in looking upon things earthly is sheer dullness when it comes to the sun. So it happens in estimating our spiritual goods. As long as we do not look beyond the earth, being quite content with our own righteousness, wisdom, and virtue, we flatter ourselves most sweetly, and fancy ourselves all but demigods. Suppose we but once begin to raise our thoughts to God, and to ponder his nature, and how completely perfect are his righteousness, wisdom, and power—the straightedge to which we must be shaped. Then, what masquerading earlier as righteousness was pleasing in us will soon grow filthy in its consummate wickedness. What wonderfully impressed us under the name of wisdom will stink in its very foolishness. What wore the face of power will prove itself the most miserable weakness. That is, what in us seems perfection itself corresponds ill to the purity of God.

I.i.3   Yet, however the knowledge of God and of ourselves may be mutually connected, the order of right teaching requires that we discuss the former first, then proceed afterward to treat the latter.

2. FAITH THE PREREQUISITE TO THE KNOWLEDGE OF GOD

I.ii.1   We shall not say that, properly speaking, God is known where there is no religion or piety.... As much in the fashioning of the universe as in the general teaching of Scripture the Lord shows himself to be simply the Creator. Then in the face of Christ [cf. 2 Cor. 4:6] he shows himself the Redeemer. Of the resulting twofold knowledge of God we shall now discuss the first aspect; the second will be dealt with in its proper place.... I call "piety" that reverence joined with love of God which the knowledge of his benefits induces.

I.ii.2   What is God? Men who pose this question are merely toying with idle speculations. It is more important for us to know of what sort he is and what is consistent with his nature. What good is it to profess with Epicurus some sort of God who has cast aside the care of the world only to amuse himself in idleness? What help is it, in short, to know a God with whom we have nothing to do?

Rather, our knowledge should serve first to teach us fear and reverence; secondly, with it as our guide and teacher, we should learn to seek every good from him, and, having received it, to credit it to his account. For how can the thought of God penetrate your mind without your realizing immediately that, since you are his handiwork, you have been made over and bound to his command by right of creation, that you owe your life to him?—that whatever you undertake, whatever you do, ought to be ascribed to him? If this be so, it now assuredly follows that your life is wickedly corrupt unless it be disposed to his service, seeing that his will ought for us to be the law by which we live....

Here indeed is pure and real religion: faith so joined with an earnest fear of God that this fear also embraces willing reverence, and carries with it such legitimate worship as is prescribed in the law. And we ought to note this fact even more diligently: all men have a vague general veneration for God, but very few really reverence him; and wherever there is great ostentation in ceremonies, sincerity of heart is rare indeed.

II

THE KNOWLEDGE
OF GOD OBSCURED

1. THE NATURAL INSTINCT FOR GOD

I.iii.1   There is within the human mind, and indeed by natural instinct, an awareness of divinity. This we take to be beyond controversy. To prevent anyone from taking refuge in the pretense of ignorance, God himself has implanted in all men a certain understanding of his divine majesty. Ever renewing its memory, he repeatedly sheds fresh drops. Since, therefore, men one and all perceive that there is a God and that he is their Maker, they are condemned by their own testimony because they have failed to honor him and to consecrate their lives to his will. . . . Therefore, since from the beginning of the world there has been no region, no city, in short, no household, that could do without religion, there lies in this a tacit confession of a sense of deity inscribed in the hearts of all.

I.iii.2   Therefore it is utterly vain for some men to say that religion was invented by the subtlety and craft of a few to hold the simple folk in thrall by this device and that those very persons who originated the worship of God for others did not in the least believe that any God existed. I confess, indeed, that in order to hold men's minds in greater subjection, clever men have devised very many things in religion by which to inspire the common folk with reverence and to strike them with terror. But they would never have achieved this if men's minds had not already been imbued with a firm conviction about God, from which the inclination toward religion springs as from a seed.

I.iii.3   Indeed, the perversity of the impious, who though
            they struggle furiously are unable to extricate them-
selves from the fear of God, is abundant testimony that this
conviction, namely, that there is some God, is naturally inborn
in all, and is fixed deep within, as it were in the very marrow. . . .
From this we conclude that it is not a doctrine that must first
be learned in school, but one of which each of us is master from
his mother's womb and which nature itself permits no one to
forget, although many strive with every nerve to this end.
. . . Therefore, it is worship of God alone that renders men
higher than the brutes, and through it alone they aspire to
immortality.

2. THIS INSTINCT OBSCURED BY IGNORANCE AND WICKEDNESS

I.iv.1   As experience shows, God has sown a seed of religion
            in all men. But scarcely one man in a hundred is met
with who fosters it, once received, in his heart, and none in
whom it ripens—much less shows fruit in season [cf. Ps. 1:3].
Besides while some may evaporate in their own superstitions
and others deliberately and wickedly desert God, yet all degenerate from the true knowledge of him. And so it happens
that no real piety remains in the world.

I.iv.2   Accordingly, we see that many, after they have
            become hardened in insolent and habitual sinning,
furiously repel all remembrance of God, although this is freely
suggested to them inwardly from the feeling of nature.

I.iv.4   They never consider God at all unless compelled to;
            and they do not come nigh until they are dragged
there despite their resistance. And not even then are they
impressed with the voluntary fear that arises out of reverence
for the divine majesty, but merely with a slavish, forced fear,
which God's judgment extorts from them. This, since they
cannot escape it, they dread even to the point of loathing.
. . . Yet that seed remains which can in no wise be uprooted:
that there is some sort of divinity; but this seed is so corrupted
that by itself it produces only the worst fruits.
    From this, my present contention is brought out with
greater certainty, that a sense of divinity is by nature engraven
on human hearts. For necessity forces from the reprobate
themselves a confession of it. In tranquil times they wittily joke

about God, indeed are facetious and garrulous in belittling his power. If any occasion for despair presses upon them, it goads them to seek him and impels their perfunctory prayers. From this it is clear that they have not been utterly ignorant of God, but that what should have come forth sooner was held back by stubbornness.

III

THE KNOWLEDGE OF GOD OBSCURED IN THE WORLD

1. GOD'S MANIFESTATION IN THE WORLD

I.v.1   The final goal of the blessed life, moreover, rests in the knowledge of God [cf. John 17:3]. Lest anyone, then, be excluded from access to happiness, he not only sowed in men's minds that seed of religion of which we have spoken but revealed himself and daily discloses himself in the whole workmanship of the universe. As a consequence, men cannot open their eyes without being compelled to see him. Indeed, his essence is incomprehensible; hence, his divineness far escapes all human perception. But upon his individual works he has engraved unmistakable marks of his glory, so clear and so prominent that even unlettered and stupid folk cannot plead the excuse of ignorance. . . . Wherever you cast your eyes, there is no spot in the universe wherein you cannot discern at least some sparks of his glory.

I.v.2   There are innumerable evidences both in heaven and on earth that declare his wonderful wisdom; not only those more recondite matters for the closer observation of which astronomy, medicine, and all natural science are intended, but also those which thrust themselves upon the sight of even the most untutored and ignorant persons, so that they cannot open their eyes without being compelled to witness them. . . . Ignorance of them prevents no one from seeing more than enough of God's workmanship in his creation to lead him to break forth in admiration of the Artificer. . . . It is, accordingly, clear that there is no one to whom the Lord does not abundantly show his wisdom.

2. OUR BLINDNESS TO GOD'S MANIFESTATION

I.v.4   Here, however, the foul ungratefulness of men is disclosed. They have within themselves a workshop
graced with God's unnumbered works and, at the same time,
a storehouse overflowing with inestimable riches. They ought,
then, to break forth into praises of him but are actually puffed
up and swollen with all the more pride. They feel in many
wonderful ways that God works in them; they are also taught,
by the very use of these things, what a great variety of gifts
they possess from his liberality. They are compelled to know—
whether they will or not—that these are the signs of divinity;
yet they conceal them within. . . .

Even today the earth sustains many monstrous spirits who,
to destroy God's name, do not hesitate to misdirect all the seed
of divinity spread abroad in human nature. How detestable, I
ask you, is this madness: that man, finding God in his body and
soul a hundred times, on this very pretense of excellence denies that there is a God? They will not say it is by chance that
they are distinct from brute creatures. Yet they set God aside,
the while using "nature," which for them is the artificer of all
things, as a cloak.

I.v.5   I confess, of course, that it can be said reverently,
provided that it proceeds from a reverent mind, that
nature is God; but because it is a harsh and improper saying,
since nature is rather the order prescribed by God, it is harmful in such weighty matters, in which special devotion is due,
to involve God confusedly in the inferior course of his works.

I.v.11   Although the Lord represents both himself and his
everlasting Kingdom in the mirror of his works with
very great clarity, such is our stupidity that we grow increas-
ingly dull toward so manifest testimonies, and they flow away
without profiting us. For with regard to the most beautiful
structure and order of the universe, how many of us are there
who, when we lift up our eyes to heaven or cast them about
through the various regions of earth, recall our minds to a
remembrance of the Creator, and do not rather, disregarding
their Author, sit idly in contemplation of his works? In fact,
with regard to those events which daily take place outside the
ordinary course of nature, how many of us do not reckon that
men are whirled and twisted about by blindly indiscriminate
fortune, rather than governed by God's providence? Sometimes we are driven by the leading and direction of these

things to contemplate God; this of necessity happens to all men. Yet after we rashly grasp a conception of some sort of divinity, straightway we fall back into the ravings or evil imaginings of our flesh, and corrupt by our vanity the pure truth of God. In one respect we are indeed unalike, because each one of us privately forges his own particular error; yet we are very much alike in that, one and all, we forsake the one true God for prodigious trifles. Not only the common folk and dull-witted men, but also the most excellent and those otherwise endowed with keen discernment, are infected with this disease.

I.v.14   It is therefore in vain that so many burning lamps shine for us in the workmanship of the universe to show forth the glory of its Author. Although they bathe us wholly in their radiance, yet they can of themselves in no way lead us into the right path. Surely they strike some sparks, but before their fuller light shines forth these are smothered. For this reason, the apostle, in that very passage where he calls the worlds the images of things invisible, adds that through faith we understand that they have been fashioned by God's word [Heb. 11:3]. He means by this that the invisible divinity is made manifest in such spectacles, but that we have not the eyes to see this unless they be illumined by the inner revelation of God through faith. . . . Therefore, although the Lord does not want for testimony while he sweetly attracts men to the knowledge of himself with many and varied kindnesses, they do not cease on this account to follow their own ways, that is, their fatal errors.

I.v.15   But although we lack the natural ability to mount up unto the pure and clear knowledge of God, all excuse is cut off because the fault of dullness is within us. And, indeed, we are not allowed thus to pretend ignorance without our conscience itself always convicting us of both baseness and ingratitude. As if this defense may properly be admitted: for a man to pretend that he lacks ears to hear the truth when there are mute creatures with more than melodious voices to declare it; or for a man to claim that he cannot see with his eyes what eyeless creatures point out to him; or for him to plead feebleness of mind when even irrational creatures give instruction! Therefore we are justly denied every excuse when we stray off as wanderers and vagrants even though everything points out the right way. But, however that may be, yet the fact that men soon corrupt the seed of the knowledge of

God, sown in their minds out of the wonderful workmanship of nature (thus preventing it from coming to a good and perfect fruit), must be imputed to their own failing; nevertheless, it is very true that we are not at all sufficiently instructed by this bare and simple testimony which the creatures render splendidly to the glory of God. For at the same time as we have enjoyed a slight taste of the divine from contemplation of the universe, having neglected the true God, we raise up in his stead dreams and specters of our own brains, and attribute to anything else than the true source the praise of righteousness, wisdom, goodness, and power. Moreover, we so obscure or overturn his daily acts by wickedly judging them that we snatch away from them their glory and from their Author his due praise.

IV

THE KNOWLEDGE OF GOD
REVEALED IN SCRIPTURE

1. SCRIPTURE THE SOURCE
OF OUR KNOWLEDGE OF GOD

I.vi.1   That brightness which is borne in upon the eyes of all
men both in heaven and on earth is more than enough
to withdraw all support from men's ingratitude—just as God,
to involve the human race in the same guilt, sets forth to all
without exception his presence portrayed in his creatures. Despite this, it is needful that another and better help be added
to direct us aright to the very Creator of the universe. It was
not in vain, then, that he added the light of his Word by which
to become known unto salvation; and he regarded as worthy
of this privilege those whom he pleased to gather more closely
and intimately to himself. . . .

Just as old or bleary-eyed men and those with weak vision,
if you thrust before them a most beautiful volume, even if they
recognize it to be some sort of writing, yet can scarcely con-
strue two words, but with the aid of spectacles will begin to
read distinctly; so Scripture, gathering up the otherwise confused knowledge of God in our minds, having dispersed our
dullness, clearly shows us the true God. This, therefore, is a
special gift, where God, to instruct the church, not merely uses
mute teachers but also opens his own most hallowed lips. Not
only does he teach the elect to look upon a god, but also shows
himself as the God upon whom they are to look. . . .

We should learn from Scripture that God, the Creator of the
universe, can by sure marks be distinguished from all the
throng of feigned gods. Then, in due order, that series will lead
us to the redemption. . . . God, the Artificer of the universe,
is made manifest to us in Scripture, and . . . what we ought to

think of him is set forth there, lest we seek some uncertain deity by devious paths.

I.vi.2   But whether God became known to the patriarchs through oracles and visions or by the work and ministry of men, he put into their minds what they should then hand down to their posterity. At any rate, there is no doubt that firm certainty of doctrine was engraved in their hearts, so that they were convinced and understood that what they had learned proceeded from God. For by his Word, God rendered faith unambiguous forever, a faith that should be superior to all opinion. Finally, in order that truth might abide forever in the world with a continuing succession of teaching and survive through all ages, the same oracles he had given to the patriarchs it was his pleasure to have recorded, as it were, on public tablets. With this intent the law was published, and the prophets afterward added as its interpreters. . . . Now, in order that true religion may shine upon us, we ought to hold that it must take its beginning from heavenly doctrine and that no one can get even the slightest taste of right and sound doctrine unless he be a pupil of Scripture.

I.vi.3   God has provided the assistance of the Word for the sake of all those to whom he has been pleased to give useful instruction because he foresaw that his likeness imprinted upon the most beautiful form of the universe would be insufficiently effective. Hence, we must strive onward by this straight path if we seriously aspire to the pure contemplation of God. We must come, I say, to the Word, where God is truly and vividly described to us from his works.

If we turn aside from the Word, as I have just now said, though we may strive with strenuous haste, yet, since we have got off the track, we shall never reach the goal. For we should so reason that the splendor of the divine countenance, which even the apostle calls "unapproachable" [1 Tim. 6:16], is for us like an inexplicable labyrinth unless we are conducted into it by the thread of the Word.

2. THE AUTHORITY OF SCRIPTURE
AND THE INTERNAL TESTIMONY
OF THE HOLY SPIRIT

I.vii.1   Before I go any farther, it is worthwhile to say something about the authority of Scripture. . . . This matter is very well worth treating more fully and weighing more carefully. . . . But a most pernicious error widely prevails that Scripture has only so much weight as is conceded to it by the consent of the church. As if the eternal and inviolable truth of God depended upon the decision of men! For they mock the Holy Spirit when they ask: Who can convince us that these writings came from God? Who can assure us that Scripture has come down whole and intact even to our very day? Who can persuade us to receive one book in reverence but to exclude another, unless the church prescribe a sure rule for all these matters? What reverence is due Scripture and what books ought to be reckoned within its canon depend, they say, upon the determination of the church. . . . Yet, if this is so, what will happen to miserable consciences seeking firm assurance of eternal life if all promises of it consist in and depend solely upon the judgment of men?

I.vii.2   If the Christian church was from the beginning founded upon the writings of the prophets and the preaching of the apostles, wherever this doctrine is found, the acceptance of it—without which the church itself would never have existed—must certainly have preceded the church. It is utterly vain, then, to pretend that the power of judging Scripture so lies with the church that its certainty depends upon churchly assent. Thus, while the church receives and gives its seal of approval to the Scriptures, it does not thereby render authentic what is otherwise doubtful or controversial. But because the church recognizes Scripture to be the truth of its own God, as a pious duty it unhesitatingly venerates Scripture. As to their question—How can we be assured that this has sprung from God unless we have recourse to the decree of the church?—it is as if someone asked: Whence will we learn to distinguish light from darkness, white from black, sweet from bitter? Indeed, Scripture exhibits fully as clear evidence of its own truth as white and black things do of their color, or sweet and bitter things do of their taste.

I.vii.4   We ought to remember what I said a bit ago: credibility of doctrine is not established until we are persuaded beyond doubt that God is its Author. Thus, the highest proof of Scripture derives in general from the fact that God in person speaks in it. The prophets and apostles do not boast either of their keenness or of anything that obtains credit for them as they speak; nor do they dwell upon rational proofs

Rather, they bring forward God's holy name, that by it the whole world may be brought into obedience to him. . . . If we desire to provide in the best way for our consciences—that they may not be perpetually beset by the instability of doubt or vacillation, and that they may not also boggle at the smallest quibbles—we ought to seek our conviction in a higher place than human reasons, judgments, or conjectures, that is, in the secret testimony of the Spirit.

But even if anyone clears God's Sacred Word from man's evil speaking, he will not at once imprint upon their hearts that certainty which piety requires. Since for unbelieving men religion seems to stand by opinion alone, they, in order not to believe anything foolishly or lightly, both wish and demand rational proof that Moses and the prophets spoke divinely. But I reply: the testimony of the Spirit is more excellent than all reason. For as God alone is a fit witness of himself in his Word, so also the Word will not find acceptance in men's hearts before it is sealed by the inward testimony of the Spirit. The same Spirit, therefore, who has spoken through the mouths of the prophets must penetrate into our hearts to persuade us that they faithfully proclaimed what had been divinely commanded.

I.vii.5   Let this point therefore stand: that those whom the Holy Spirit has inwardly taught truly rest upon Scripture, and that Scripture indeed is self-authenticated; hence, it is not right to subject it to proof and reasoning. And the certainty it deserves with us, it attains by the testimony of the Spirit. For even if it wins reverence for itself by its own majesty, it seriously affects us only when it is sealed upon our hearts through the Spirit. Therefore, illumined by his power, we believe neither by our own nor by anyone else's judgment that Scripture is from God; but above human judgment we affirm with utter certainty (just as if we were gazing upon the majesty of God himself) that it has flowed to us from the very mouth of God by the ministry of men. . . . Such, then, is a conviction that requires no reasons; such, a knowledge with which the best reason agrees—in which the mind truly reposes more securely and constantly than in any reasons; such, finally, a feeling that can be born only of heavenly revelation. I speak of nothing other than what each believer experiences within himself—though my words fall far beneath a just explanation of the matter. . . . The only true faith is that which the Spirit of God seals in our hearts. . . . Whenever, then, the fewness of believers disturbs us, let the converse come to mind, that only those to whom it is given can comprehend the mysteries of God [cf. Matt. 13:11].

I.viii.13   Scripture will ultimately suffice for a saving knowledge of God only when its certainty is founded upon the inward persuasion of the Holy Spirit. Indeed, these human testimonies which exist to confirm it will not be vain if, as secondary aids to our feebleness, they follow that chief and highest testimony. But those who wish to prove to unbelievers that Scripture is the Word of God are acting foolishly, for only by faith can this be known. Augustine therefore justly warns that godliness and peace of mind ought to come first if a man is to understand anything of such great matters.

3. THE ADEQUACY OF SCRIPTURE

I.ix.1   Those who, having forsaken Scripture, imagine some way or other of reaching God, ought to be thought of as not so much gripped by error as carried away with frenzy. For of late, certain giddy men have arisen who, with great haughtiness exalting the teaching office of the Spirit, despise all reading and laugh at the simplicity of those who, as they express it, still follow the dead and killing letter.... What devilish madness is it to pretend that the use of Scripture, which leads the children of God even to the final goal, is fleeting or temporal? .... Therefore the Spirit, promised to us, has not the task of inventing new and unheard-of revelations, or of forging a new kind of doctrine, to lead us away from the received doctrine of the gospel, but of sealing our minds with that very doctrine which is commended by the gospel.

I.ix.2   From this we readily understand that we ought zealously to apply ourselves both to read and to hearken to Scripture if indeed we want to receive any gain and benefit from the Spirit of God.... He is the Author of the Scriptures: he cannot vary and differ from himself. Hence he must ever remain just as he once revealed himself there. This is no affront to him, unless perchance we consider it honorable for him to decline or degenerate from himself.

I.ix.3   For by a kind of mutual bond the Lord has joined together the certainty of his Word and of his Spirit.... God did not bring forth his Word among men for the sake of a momentary display, intending at the coming of his Spirit to abolish it. Rather, he sent down the same Spirit by whose power he had dispensed the Word, to complete his work by the efficacious confirmation of the Word. . . . In this manner Christ opened the minds of two of his disciples [Luke 24:27, 45], not that they should cast away the Scriptures and become wise of themselves, but that they should know the Scriptures. . . .

What say these fanatics, swollen with pride, who consider this the one excellent illumination when, carelessly forsaking and bidding farewell to God's Word, they, no less confidently than boldly, seize upon whatever they may have conceived while snoring? Certainly a far different sobriety befits the children of God, who just as they see themselves, without the Spirit of God, bereft of the whole light of truth, so are not unaware that the Word is the instrument by which the Lord dispenses the illumination of his Spirit to believers. For they know no other Spirit than him who dwelt and spoke in the apostles, and by whose oracles they are continually recalled to the hearing of the Word.

V

THE NATURE
AND ATTRIBUTES OF GOD

I.x.1   At present let it be enough to grasp how God, the Maker of heaven and earth, governs the universe founded by him. Indeed, both his fatherly goodness and his beneficently inclined will are repeatedly extolled; and examples of his severity are given, which show him to be the righteous avenger of evil deeds, especially where his forbearance toward the obstinate is of no effect.

I.x.2   For when Moses described the image, he obviously meant to tell briefly whatever was right for men to know about him. "Jehovah," he says, "Jehovah, a merciful and gracious God, patient and of much compassion, and true, who keepest mercy for thousands, who takest away iniquity and transgression, . . . in whose presence the innocent will not be innocent, who visitest the iniquity of the fathers upon the children and the children's children" [Ex. 34:6–7; cf. Vg.]. Here let us observe that his eternity and his self-existence are announced by that wonderful name twice repeated. Thereupon his powers are mentioned, by which he is shown to us not as he is in himself, but as he is toward us: so that this recognition of him consists more in living experience than in vain and high-flown speculation. Now we hear the same powers enumerated there that we have noted as shining in heaven and earth: kindness, goodness, mercy, justice, judgment, and truth. For power and might are contained under the title *Elohim.*

By the same epithets also the prophets designate him when they wish to display his holy name to the full. That we may not be compelled to assemble many instances, at present let one psalm [Ps. 145] suffice for us, in which the sum of all his powers is so precisely reckoned up that nothing would seem to have been omitted [esp. Ps. 145:5]. . . .

Certainly these three things are especially necessary for us to know: mercy, on which alone the salvation of us all rests; judgment, which is daily exercised against wrongdoers, and in even greater severity awaits them to their everlasting ruin; justice, whereby believers are preserved, and are most tenderly nourished. When these are understood, the prophecy witnesses that you have abundant reason to glory in God. Yet neither his truth, nor power, nor holiness, nor goodness is thus overlooked. For how could we have the requisite knowledge of his justice, mercy, and judgment unless that knowledge rested upon his unbending truth? And without understanding his power, how could we believe that he rules the earth in judgment and justice? But whence comes his mercy save from his goodness?

VI

THE TRINITY

1. THE DOCTRINE STATED

I.xiii.2 [God] so proclaims himself the sole God as to offer himself to be contemplated clearly in three persons. Unless we grasp these, only the bare and empty name of God flits about in our brains, to the exclusion of the true God. Again, lest anyone imagine that God is threefold, or think God's simple essence to be torn into three persons, we must here seek a short and easy definition to free us from all error. . . .

There are in God three hypostases. Since the Latins can express the same concept by the word "person," to wrangle over this clear matter is undue squeamishness and even obstinacy. If anyone longs to translate word for word, let him use "subsistence." Many have used "substance" in the same sense. Nor was the word "person" in use only among the Latins, for the Greeks, perhaps to testify their agreement, taught that there are three *prosōpa* in God. Although they, whether Greek or Latin, differ among themselves over the word, yet they quite agree in the essential matter.

I.xiii.3 Now, although the heretics rail at the word "person," or certain squeamish men cry out against admitting a term fashioned by the human mind, they cannot shake our conviction that three are spoken of, each of which is entirely God, yet that there is not more than one God. What wickedness, then, it is to disapprove of words that explain nothing else than what is attested and sealed by Scripture!

It would be enough, they say, to confine within the limits of Scripture not only our thoughts but also our words, rather than scatter foreign terms about, which would become seedbeds of dissension and strife. For thus are we wearied with quarreling over words, thus by bickering do we lose the truth, thus by hateful wrangling do we destroy love. If they call a foreign word one that cannot be shown to stand written syllable by syllable in Scripture, they are indeed imposing upon us an unjust law which condemns all interpretation not patched together out of the fabric of Scripture. . . .

We ought to seek from Scripture a sure rule for both thinking and speaking, to which both the thoughts of our minds and the words of our mouths should be conformed. But what prevents us from explaining in clearer words those matters in Scripture which perplex and hinder our understanding, yet which conscientiously and faithfully serve the truth of Scripture itself, and are made use of sparingly and modestly and on due occasion?

I.xiii.5   If, therefore, these terms were not rashly invented, we ought to beware lest by repudiating them we be accused of overweening rashness. Indeed, I could wish they were buried, if only among all men this faith were agreed on: that Father and Son and Spirit are one God, yet the Son is not the Father, nor the Spirit the Son, but that they are differentiated by a peculiar quality.

Really, I am not, indeed, such a stickler as to battle doggedly over mere words. For I note that the ancients, who otherwise speak very reverently concerning these matters, agree neither among themselves nor even at all times individually with themselves. . . .

If anxious superstition so constrains anyone that he cannot bear these terms, yet no one could now deny, even if he were to burst, that when we hear "one" we ought to understand "unity of substance"; when we hear "three in one essence," the persons in this trinity are meant. When this is confessed without guile, we need not dally over words. But I have long since and repeatedly been experiencing that all who persistently quarrel over words nurse a secret poison. As a consequence, it is more expedient to challenge them deliberately than speak more obscurely to please them.

2. THE DISTINCTION BETWEEN THE PERSONS

I.xiii.6   But laying aside disputation over terms, I shall proceed to speak of the thing itself: "Person," therefore, I call a "subsistence" in God's essence, which, while related to the others, is distinguished by an incommunicable quality. By the term "subsistence" we would understand something different from "essence." For if the Word were simply God, and yet possessed no other characteristic mark, John would wrongly have said that the Word was always with God [John 1:1]. When immediately after he adds that the Word was also God himself, he recalls us to the essence as a unity. But because he could not be with God without residing in the Father, hence emerges the idea of a subsistence, which, even though it has been joined with the essence by a common bond and cannot be separated from it, yet has a special mark whereby it is distinguished from it. Now, of the three subsistences I say that each one, while related to the others, is distinguished by a special quality. This "relation" is here distinctly expressed: because where simple and indefinite mention is made of God, this name pertains no less to the Son and the Spirit than to the Father. But as soon as the Father is compared with the Son, the character of each distinguishes the one from the other. Thirdly, whatever is proper to each individually, I maintain to be incommunicable because whatever is attributed to the Father as a distinguishing mark cannot agree with, or be transferred to, the Son. Nor am I displeased with Tertullian's definition, provided it be taken in the right sense, that there is a kind of distribution or economy in God which has no effect on the unity of essence.

I.xiii.17 Scripture sets forth a distinction of the Father from the Word, and of the Word from the Spirit. Yet the greatness of the mystery warns us how much reverence and sobriety we ought to use in investigating this. And that passage in Gregory of Nazianzus vastly delights me: "I cannot think on the one without quickly being encircled by the splendor of the three; nor can I discern the three without being straightway carried back to the one." Let us not, then, be led to imagine a trinity of persons that keeps our thoughts distracted and does not at once lead them back to that unity. Indeed, the words "Father," "Son," and "Spirit" imply a real distinction—let no one think that these titles, whereby God is variously designated from his works, are empty—but a distinction, not a division. The passages that we have already cited [e.g., Zech. 13:7] show that the Son has a character distinct from the Father, because the Word would not have been with God unless he were another than the Father, nor would he have had his glory with the Father were he not distinct from the Father. In like manner he distinguishes the Father from himself when he says that there is another who bears witness to him [John 5:32; 8:16;

and elsewhere]. And with this agrees what is said elsewhere: that the Father created all things through the Word [John 1:3; Heb. 11:3]. This he could not have done without being somehow distinct from the Word. Furthermore, it was not the Father who descended upon the earth, but he who went forth from the Father; the Father did not die, nor did he arise again, but rather he who had been sent by the Father. Nor did this distinction have its beginning from the time that he assumed flesh, but before this also it is manifest that he was the only-begotten "in the bosom of the Father" [John 1:18]. For who would take upon himself to assert that the Son did not enter into the bosom of the Father until he descended from heaven to assume humanity? Therefore he was in the bosom of the Father before, and held his own glory in the presence of the Father [John 17:5]. Christ implies the distinction of the Holy Spirit from the Father when he says that the Holy Spirit proceeds from the Father [John 15:26; cf. 14:26]. He implies the distinction of the Holy Spirit from himself as often as he calls the Spirit "another," as when he announces that he will send another Comforter [John 14:16], and often elsewhere.

3. THE DOCTRINE EXPLAINED

I.xiii.18   I really do not know whether it is expedient to borrow comparisons from human affairs to express the force of this distinction. . . . Nevertheless, it is not fitting to suppress the distinction that we observe to be expressed in Scripture. It is this: to the Father is attributed the beginning of activity, and the fountain and wellspring of all things; to the Son, wisdom, counsel, and the ordered disposition of all things; but to the Spirit is assigned the power and efficacy of that activity. Indeed, although the eternity of the Father is also the eternity of the Son and the Spirit, since God could never exist apart from his wisdom and power, and we must not seek in eternity a *before* or an *after*, nevertheless the observance of an order is not meaningless or superfluous, when the Father is thought of as first, then from him the Son, and finally from both the Spirit. For the mind of each human being is naturally inclined to contemplate God first, then the wisdom coming forth from him, and lastly the power whereby he executes the decrees of his plan. For this reason, the Son is said to come forth from the Father alone; the Spirit, from the Father and the Son at the same time.

I.xiii.19   By these appellations which set forth the distinction
(says Augustine) is signified their mutual relationships
and not the very substance by which they are one. In this sense
the opinions of the ancients are to be harmonized, which otherwise would seem somewhat to clash. Sometimes, indeed,
they teach that the Father is the beginning of the Son; sometimes they declare that the Son has both divinity and essence
from himself, and thus has one beginning with the Father.
Augustine well and clearly expresses the cause of this diversity
in another place, when he speaks as follows: "Christ with respect to himself is called God; with respect to the Father, Son.
Again, the Father with respect to himself is called God; with
respect to the Son, Father. In so far as he is called Father with
respect to the Son, he is not the Son; in so far as he is called
the Son with respect to the Father, he is not the Father; in so
far as he is called both Father with respect to himself, and Son
with respect to himself, he is the same God."

I.xiii.20   Therefore, let those who dearly love soberness, and
who will be content with the measure of faith, receive
in brief form what is useful to know: namely, that, when we
profess to believe in one God, under the name of God is understood a single, simple essence, in which we comprehend three
persons, or hypostases. Therefore, whenever the name of God
is mentioned without particularization, there are designated
no less the Son and the Spirit than the Father; but where the
Son is joined to the Father, then the relation of the two enters
in; and so we distinguish among the persons.

I.xiii.22   The essence of the one God is simple and undivided,
and . . . it belongs to the Father, the Son, and the
Spirit; and on the other hand . . . by a certain characteristic the
Father differs from the Son, and the Son from the Spirit.

I.xiii.29   I trust that the whole sum of this doctrine has been
faithfully explained, if my readers will impose a limit
upon their curiosity, and not seek out for themselves more
eagerly than is proper troublesome and perplexed disputa-
tions. For I suspect that those who intemperately delight in
speculation will not be at all satisfied.

VII

THE CREATION OF THE WORLD

1. THE CREATOR AND CREATION

I.xiv.1 When a certain shameless fellow mockingly asked a pious old man what God had done before the creation of the world, the latter aptly countered that he had been building hell for the curious.

I.xiv.20 That we may apprehend with true faith what it profits us to know of God, it is important for us to grasp first the history of the creation of the universe, as it has been set forth briefly by Moses [Gen., chs. 1 and 2]. . . . God by the power of his Word and Spirit created heaven and earth out of nothing; that thereupon he brought forth living beings and inanimate things of every kind, that in a wonderful series he distinguished an innumerable variety of things, that he endowed each kind with its own nature, assigned functions, appointed places and stations; and that, although all were subject to corruption, he nevertheless provided for the preservation of each species until the Last Day. We shall likewise learn that he nourishes some in secret ways, and, as it were, from time to time instills new vigor into them; on others he has conferred the power of propagating, lest by their death the entire species perish; that he has so wonderfully adorned heaven and earth with as unlimited abundance, variety, and beauty of all things as could possibly be, quite like a spacious and splendid house, provided and filled with the most exquisite and at the same time most abundant furnishings. Finally, we shall learn that in forming man and in adorning him with such goodly beauty, and with such great and numerous gifts, he put him forth as the most excellent example of his works. But since it is not my purpose to recount the creation of the universe, let it be enough for me to have touched upon these few matters again in passing.

I.xiv.21   If we chose to explain in a fitting manner how God's inestimable wisdom, power, justice, and goodness shine forth in the fashioning of the universe, no splendor, no ornament of speech, would be equal to an act of such great magnitude. . . . But because our purpose here is to teach, it is proper for us to omit those matters which require long harangue. Therefore, to be brief, let all readers know that they have with true faith apprehended what it is for God to be Creator of heaven and earth, if they first of all follow the universal rule, not to pass over in ungrateful thoughtlessness or forgetfulness those conspicious powers which God shows forth in his creatures, and then learn so to apply it to themselves that their very hearts are touched. The first part of the rule is exemplified when we reflect upon the greatness of the Artificer who stationed, arranged, and fitted together the starry host of heaven in such wonderful order that nothing more beautiful in appearance can be imagined. . . . It is so too when we observe his power in sustaining so great a mass, in governing the swiftly revolving heavenly system, and the like. . . . If I decide to set forth the whole matter in my discourse, there will be no end. For there are as many miracles of divine power, as many tokens of goodness, and as many proofs of wisdom, as there are kinds of things in the universe, indeed, as there are things either great or small.

2. THE RELIGIOUS SIGNIFICANCE OF CREATION

I.xiv.22   There remains the second part of the rule, more closely related to faith. It is to recognize that God has destined all things for our good and salvation but at the same time to feel his power and grace in ourselves and in the great benefits he has conferred upon us, and so bestir ourselves to trust, invoke, praise, and love him. . . .

Whenever we call God the Creator of heaven and earth, let us at the same time bear in mind that the dispensation of all those things which he has made is in his own hand and power and that we are indeed his children, whom he has received into his faithful protection to nourish and educate. We are therefore to await the fullness of all good things from him alone and to trust completely that he will never leave us destitute of what we need for salvation, and to hang our hopes on none but him! We are therefore, also, to petition him for whatever we desire; and we are to recognize as a blessing from him, and thankfully to acknowledge, every benefit that falls to our share. So, invited by the great sweetness of his beneficence and goodness, let us study to love and serve him with all our heart.

VIII

THE HUMAN CREATION

1. THE IMAGE OF GOD

I.xv.1   We must now speak of the creation of man: not only because among all God's works here is the noblest and most remarkable example of his justice, wisdom, and goodness; but because, as we said at the beginning, we cannot have a clear and complete knowledge of God unless it is accompanied by a corresponding knowledge of ourselves. This knowledge of ourselves is twofold: namely, to know what we were like when we were first created and what our condition became after the fall of Adam. While it would be of little benefit to understand our creation unless we recognized in this sad ruin what our nature in its corruption and deformity is like, we shall nevertheless be content for the moment with the description of our originally upright nature. And to be sure, before we come to the miserable condition of man to which he is now subjected, it is worth-while to know what he was like when first created. . . . Afterward, in the proper place, we shall see how far away men are from the purity that was bestowed upon Adam.

I.xv.2   That man consists of a soul and a body ought to be beyond controversy. Now I understand by the term "soul" an immortal yet created essence, which is his nobler part.

I.xv.3   For although God's glory shines forth in the outer man, yet there is no doubt that the proper seat of his image is in the soul. I do not deny, indeed, that our outward form, in so far as it distinguishes and separates us from brute animals, at the same time more closely joins us to God. And if anyone wishes to include under "image of God" the fact that, "while all other living things being bent over look earthward, man has been given a face uplifted, bidden to gaze heavenward and to raise his countenance to the stars," I shall not contend too strongly—provided it be regarded as a settled principle that the image of God, which is seen or glows in these outward marks, is spiritual.

There is no slight quarrel over "image" and "likeness" when interpreters seek a nonexistent difference between these two words, except that "likeness" has been added by way of explanation. . . . The likeness of God extends to the whole excellence by which man's nature towers over all the kinds of living creatures. Accordingly, the integrity with which Adam was endowed is expressed by this word [image], when he had full possession of right understanding, when he had his affections kept within the bounds of reason, all his senses tempered in right order, and he truly referred his excellence to exceptional gifts bestowed upon him by his Maker.

I.xv.4 Nevertheless, it seems that we do not have a full definition of "image" if we do not see more plainly those faculties in which man excels, and in which he ought to be thought the reflection of God's glory. That, indeed, can be nowhere better recognized than from the restoration of his corrupted nature. There is no doubt that Adam, when he fell from his state, was by this defection alienated from God. Therefore, even though we grant that God's image was not totally annihilated and destroyed in him, yet it was so corrupted that whatever remains is frightful deformity. Consequently, the beginning of our recovery of salvation is in that restoration which we obtain through Christ, who also is called the Second Adam for the reason that he restores us to true and complete integrity. . . . The end of regeneration is that Christ should reform us to God's image. . . . Now we are to see what Paul chiefly comprehends under this renewal. In the first place he posits knowledge, then pure righteousness and holiness. From this we infer that, to begin with, God's image was visible in the light of the mind, in the uprightness of the heart, and in the soundness of all the parts.

2. THE ERROR OF PANTHEISM

I.xv.5 But before we go farther, we must confront the delusion of the Manichees, which Servetus has tried to introduce once more in this age. Because it is said that God breathed the breath of life upon man's face [Gen. 2:7], they thought the soul to be a derivative of God's substance, as if some portion of immeasurable divinity had flowed into man. Yet it is easy to point out quickly what crass and foul absurdities this devilish error drags in its train. For if man's soul be from the essence of God through derivation, it will follow that God's nature is subject not only to change and passions, but also to ignorance, wicked desires, infirmity, and all manner of vices. Nothing is more inconstant than man. Contrary motions stir up and variously distract his soul. Repeatedly he is led astray by ignorance. He yields, overcome by the slightest temptation. We know his mind to be a sink and lurking place for every sort of filth. All these things one must attribute to God's nature, if we understand the soul to be from God's essence, or to be a secret inflowing of divinity. Who would not shudder at this monstrous thing? Indeed, Paul truly quotes Aratus that we are God's offspring [Acts 17:28], but in quality, not in essence, inasmuch as he, indeed, adorned us with divine gifts. Meanwhile, to tear apart the essence of the Creator so that everyone may possess a part of it is utter folly. Therefore we must take it to be a fact that souls, although the image of God be engraved upon them, are just as much created as angels are. But creation is not inpouring, but the beginning of essence out of nothing.

3. THE NATURE OF THE SOUL

I.xv.6   It would be foolish to seek a definition of "soul" from the philosophers.

I.xv.7   The philosophers, ignorant of the corruption of nature that originated from the penalty for man's defection, mistakenly confuse two very diverse states of man. Thus let us, therefore, hold—as indeed is suitable to our present purpose—that the human soul consists of two faculties, understanding and will. Let the office, moreover, of understanding be to distinguish between objects, as each seems worthy of approval or disapproval; while that of the will, to choose and follow what the understanding pronounces good, but to reject and flee what it disapproves. . . .

Not to entangle ourselves in useless questions, let it be enough for us that the understanding is, as it were, the leader and governor of the soul; and that the will is always mindful of the bidding of the understanding, and in its own desires awaits the judgment of the understanding. . . . Here we wish to say only this, that no power can be found in the soul that does not duly have reference to one or the other of these members.

I.xv.8   God provided man's soul with a mind, by which to distinguish good from evil, right from wrong; and, with the light of reason as guide, to distinguish what should be followed from what should be avoided. . . . To this he joined the will, under whose control is choice. Man in his first condition excelled in these pre-eminent endowments. . . .

In this integrity man by free will had the power, if he so willed, to attain eternal life. Here it would be out of place to raise the question of God's secret predestination because our present subject is not what can happen or not, but what man's nature was like. Therefore Adam could have stood if he wished, seeing that he fell solely by his own will. . . .

Now we need bear only this in mind: man was far different at the first creation from his whole posterity, who, deriving their origin from him in his corrupted state, have contracted from him a hereditary taint. . . . But to quarrel with God on this precise point, as if he ought to have conferred this upon man, is more than iniquitous, inasmuch as it was in his own choice to give whatever he pleased. But the reason he did not sustain man by the virtue of perseverance lies hidden in his plan; sobriety is for us the part of wisdom.

IX

PROVIDENCE

1. PROVIDENCE OPPOSED TO FORTUNE, FATE, AND CHANCE

I.xvi.1   To make God a momentary Creator, who once for all
finished his work, would be cold and barren, and we
must differ from profane men especially in that we see the
presence of divine power shining as much in the continuing
state of the universe as in its inception. . . .

Faith ought to penetrate more deeply, namely, having
found him Creator of all, forthwith to conclude he is also everlasting Governor and Preserver—not only in that he drives the
celestial frame as well as its several parts by a universal motion,
but also in that he sustains, nourishes, and cares for, everything
he has made, even to the least sparrow [cf. Matt. 10:29]. . . . All
parts of the universe are quickened by God's secret inspiration.

I.xvi.2   That this difference may better appear, we must
know that God's providence, as it is taught in Scripture, is opposed to fortune and fortuitous happenings. Now it
has been commonly accepted in all ages, and almost all mortals
hold the same opinion today, that all things come about
through chance. What we ought to believe concerning providence is by this depraved opinion most certainly not only
beclouded, but almost buried. Suppose a man falls among
thieves, or wild beasts; is shipwrecked at sea by a sudden gale;
is killed by a falling house or tree. Suppose another man wandering through the desert finds help in his straits; having been
tossed by the waves, reaches harbor; miraculously escapes
death by a finger's breadth. Carnal reason ascribes all such

happenings, whether prosperous or adverse, to fortune. But anyone who has been taught by Christ's lips that all the hairs of his head are numbered [Matt. 10:30] will look farther afield for a cause, and will consider that all events are governed by God's secret plan.

I.xvi.8   Those who wish to cast odium upon this doctrine defame it as the Stoics' dogma of fate. This charge was once hurled at Augustine. Even though we are unwilling to quarrel over words, yet we do not admit the word "fate," both because it is one of those words whose profane novelties Paul teaches us to avoid [1 Tim. 6:20], and because men try by the odium it incurs to oppress God's truth. Indeed, we are falsely and maliciously charged with this very dogma. We do not, with the Stoics, contrive a necessity out of the perpetual connection and intimately related series of causes, which is contained in nature; but we make God the ruler and governor of all things, who in accordance with his wisdom has from the farthest limit of eternity decreed what he was going to do, and now by his might carries out what he has decreed. From this we declare that not only heaven and earth and the inanimate creatures, but also the plans and intentions of men, are so governed by his providence that they are borne by it straight to their appointed end.

I.xvi.9   Yet since the sluggishness of our mind lies far beneath the height of God's providence, we must employ a distinction to lift it up. Therefore I shall put it this way: however all things may be ordained by God's plan, according to a sure dispensation, for us they are fortuitous. Not that we think that fortune rules the world and men, tumbling all things at random up and down, for it is fitting that this folly be absent from the Christian's breast! But since the order, reason, end, and necessity of those things which happen for the most part lie hidden in God's purpose, and are not apprehended by human opinon, those things, which it is certain take place by God's will, are in a sense fortuitous.

2. THE RELIGIOUS SIGNIFICANCE OF PROVIDENCE

I.xvii.1   As men's dispositions are inclined to vain subtleties, any who do not hold fast to a good and right use of this doctrine can hardly avoid entangling themselves in inscrutable difficulties. Therefore it is expedient here to discuss briefly to what end Scripture teaches that all things are divinely ordained.

Three things, indeed, are to be noted. First, God's providence must be considered with regard to the future as well as the past. Secondly, it is the determinative principle of all things in such a way that sometimes it works through an intermediary, sometimes without an intermediary, sometimes contrary to every intermediary. Finally, it strives to the end that God may reveal his concern for the whole human race, but especially his vigilance in ruling the church, which he deigns to watch more closely. . . . But we must so cherish moderation that we do not try to make God render account to us, but so reverence his secret judgments as to consider his will the truly just cause of all things.

I.xvii.2   Therefore no one will weigh God's providence properly and profitably but him who considers that his business is with his Maker and the Framer of the universe, and with becoming humility submits himself to fear and reverence.

I.xvii.3   All who will compose themselves to this moderation will not murmur against God on account of their adversities in time past, nor lay the blame for their own wickedness upon him. . . . But rather let them inquire and learn from Scripture what is pleasing to God so that they may strive toward this under the Spirit's guidance. At the same time, being ready to follow God wherever he calls, they will show in very truth that nothing is more profitable than the knowledge of this doctrine.

I.xvii.4   He who has set the limits to our life has at the same time entrusted to us its care; he has provided means and helps to preserve it; he has also made us able to foresee dangers; that they may not overwhelm us unaware, he has offered precautions and remedies. Now it is very clear what our duty is: thus, if the Lord has committed to us the protection of our life, our duty is to protect it; if he offers helps, to use them; if he forewarns us of dangers, not to plunge headlong; if he makes remedies available, not to neglect them. . . . The Lord has inspired in men the arts of taking counsel and caution, by which to comply with his providence in the preservation of life itself: Just as, on the contrary, by neglect and slothfulness they bring upon themselves the ills that he has laid upon them.

I.xvii.5   A man, having learned of His will, obeys God in striving toward the goal to which he is called by that same
will. From what source do we learn but from his Word? In such fashion we must in our deeds search out God's will which he declares through his Word. God requires of us only what he commands. If we contrive anything against his command-ment, it is not obedience but obstinacy and transgression.

BOOK TWO

SIN AND JESUS CHRIST
THE REDEEMER

X

ORIGINAL SIN

1. THE FACT OF SIN

II.i.1 With good reason the ancient proverb strongly recommended knowledge of self to man. For if it is considered disgraceful for us not to know all that pertains to the business of human life, even more detestable is our ignorance of ourselves, by which, when making decisions in necessary matters, we miserably deceive and even blind ourselves! . . . But knowledge of ourselves lies first in considering what we were given at creation and how generously God continues his favor toward us, in order to know how great our natural excellence would be if only it had remained unblemished; yet at the same time to bear in mind that there is in us nothing of our own, but that we hold on sufferance whatever God has bestowed upon us. Hence we are ever dependent on him. Secondly, to call to mind our miserable condition after Adam's fall; the awareness of which, when all our boasting and self-assurance are laid low, should truly humble us and overwhelm us with shame.

II.i.2 Here, then, is what God's truth requires us to seek in examining ourselves: it requires the kind of knowledge that will strip us of all confidence in our own ability, deprive us of all occasion for boasting, and lead us to submission. We ought to keep this rule if we wish to reach the true goal of both wisdom and action. I am quite aware how much more pleasing is that principle which invites us to weigh our good traits rather than to look upon our miserable want and dishonor, which ought to overwhelm us with shame. There is, indeed, nothing that man's nature seeks more eagerly than to be flattered. Accordingly, when his nature becomes aware that its gifts are highly esteemed, it tends to be unduly credulous about them. It is thus no wonder that the majority of men have erred so perniciously in this respect. For, since blind self-love is innate in all mortals, they are most freely persuaded that nothing inheres in themselves that deserves to be considered hateful. Thus even with no outside support the utterly vain opinion generally obtains credence that man is abundantly sufficient of himself to lead a good and blessed life.

II.i.3   Let us divide the knowledge that man ought to have of himself. First, he should consider for what purpose he was created and endowed with no mean gifts. By this knowledge he should arouse himself to meditation upon divine worship and the future life. Secondly, he should weigh his own abilities—or rather, lack of abilities. When he perceives this lack, he should lie prostrate in extreme confusion, so to speak, reduced to nought. The first consideration tends to make him recognize the nature of his duty; the second, the extent of his ability to carry it out.

2. THE NATURE OF SIN

II.1.4   Because what God so severely punished must have been no light sin but a detestable crime, we must consider what kind of sin there was in Adam's desertion that enkindled God's fearful vengeance against the whole of mankind. . . . Adam was denied the tree of the knowledge of good and evil to test his obedience and prove that he was willingly under God's command. . . . Augustine speaks rightly when he declares that pride was the beginning of all evils. For if ambition had not raised man higher than was meet and right, he could have remained in his original state. . . . Disobedience was the beginning of the Fall. This Paul also confirms, teaching that all were lost through the disobedience of one man [Rom. 5:19]. . . . Unfaithfulness, then, was the root of the Fall. But thereafter ambition and pride, together with ungratefulness, arose, because Adam by seeking more than was granted him shamefully spurned God's great bounty, which had been lavished upon him.

II.i.5   As it was the spiritual life of Adam to remain united and bound to his Maker, so estrangement from him was the death of his soul. Nor is it any wonder that he consigned his race to ruin by his rebellion when he perverted the whole order of nature in heaven and on earth. . . . Therefore, after the heavenly image was obliterated in him, he was not the only one to suffer this punishment—that, in place of wisdom, virtue, holiness, truth, and justice, with which adornments he had been clad, there came forth the most filthy plagues, blindness, impotence, impurity, vanity, and injustice—but he also entangled and immersed his offspring in the same miseries. This is the inherited corruption, which the church fathers termed "original sin," meaning by the word "sin" the depravation of a nature previously good and pure. . . .

When it was shown by the clear testimony of Scripture that sin was transmitted from the first man to all his posterity [Rom. 5:12], Pelagius quibbled that it was transmitted through imitation, not propagation. Therefore, good men (and Augustine above the rest) labored to show us that we are corrupted not by derived wickedness, but that we bear inborn defect from our mother's womb. . . . Therefore all of us, who have descended from impure seed, are born infected with the contagion of sin. In fact, before we saw the light of this life we were soiled and spotted in God's sight.

II.1.8 So that these remarks may not be made concerning an uncertain and unknown matter, let us define original sin. It is not my intention to investigate the several definitions proposed by various writers, but simply to bring forward the one that appears to me most in accordance with truth. Original sin, therefore, seems to be a hereditary depravity and corruption of our nature, diffused into all parts of the soul, which first makes us liable to God's wrath, then also brings forth in us those works which Scripture calls "works of the flesh" [Gal. 5:19]. . . . For, since it is said that we became subject to God's judgment through Adam's sin, we are to understand it not as if we, guiltless and undeserving, bore the guilt of his offense but in the sense that, since we through his transgression have become entangled in the curse, he is said to have made us guilty.

II.1.10 Now away with those persons who dare write God's name upon their faults, because we declare that men are vicious by nature! They perversely search out God's handiwork in their own pollution, when they ought rather to have sought it in that unimpaired and uncorrupted nature of Adam. Our destruction, therefore, comes from the guilt of our flesh, not from God, inasmuch as we have perished solely because we have degenerated from our original condition. Let no one grumble here that God could have provided better for our salvation if he had forestalled Adam's fall. Pious minds ought to loathe this objection, because it manifests inordinate curiosity.

XI

SIN AND THE FREEDOM
OF THE WILL

1. THE WILL A SLAVE TO SIN

II.ii.1   When man has been taught that no good thing remains in his power, and that he is hedged about on all sides by most miserable necessity, in spite of this he should nevertheless be instructed to aspire to a good of which he is empty, to a freedom of which he has been deprived. In fact, he may thus be more sharply aroused from inactivity than if it were supposed that he was endowed with the highest virtues. Everyone sees how necessary this second point is. I observe that too many persons have doubts about the first point. For since this is an undoubted fact, that nothing of his own ought to be taken away from man, it ought to be clearly evident how important it is for him to be barred from false boasting.

II.ii.6   If this be admitted, it will be indisputable that free will is not sufficient to enable man to do good works, unless he be helped by grace, indeed by special grace, which only the elect receive through regeneration.

II.ii.7   Man will then be spoken of as having this sort of free decision, not because he has free choice equally of good and evil, but because he acts wickedly by will, not by compulsion. Well put, indeed, but what purpose is served by labeling with a proud name such a slight thing? A noble freedom, indeed—for man not to be forced to serve sin, yet to be such a willing slave that his will is bound by the fetters of sin! Indeed, I abhor contentions about words, with which the church is harassed to no purpose. But I have scrupulously resolved to avoid those words which signify something absurd, especially where pernicious error is involved. But how few men are there, I ask, who when they hear free will attributed to man do not immediately conceive him to be master of both his own mind and will, able of his own power to turn himself toward either good or evil?

II.ii.8   Now, if the authority of the fathers has weight with us, they indeed have the word constantly on their lips, yet at the same time they declare what it connotes to them. First of all, there is Augustine, who does not hesitate to call it "unfree." Elsewhere he is angry toward those who deny that the will is free; but he states his main reason in these words: "Only let no one so dare to deny the decision of the will as to wish to excuse sin." Yet elsewhere he plainly confesses that "without the Spirit man's will is not free, since it has been laid under by shackling and conquering desires." . . . Therefore in another passage, after showing that free will is established through grace, he bitterly inveighs against those who claim it for themselves without grace. "Why then," he says, "do miserable men either dare to boast of free will before they have been freed, or of their powers, if they have already been freed? And they do not heed the fact that in the term 'free will' freedom seems to be implied. 'Now where the Spirit of the Lord is, there is freedom' " [2 Cor. 3:17]. . . . If anyone, then, can use this word without understanding it in a bad sense, I shall not trouble him on this account. But I hold that because it cannot be retained without great peril, it will, on the contrary, be a great boon for the church if it be abolished. I prefer not to use it myself, and I should like others, if they seek my advice, to avoid it.

2. TOTAL DEPRAVITY

II.iii.2   The apostle [Paul], when he wishes to cast down the arrogance of humankind, does so by these testimonies: " 'No one is righteous, no one understands, no one seeks God. All have turned aside, together they have become unprofitable; no one does good, not even one' [Ps. 14:1–3; 53:1–3]. 'Their throat is an open grave, they use their tongues deceitfully' [Ps. 5:9]. 'The venom of asps is under their lips' [Ps. 140:3]. 'Their mouth is full of cursing and bitterness' [Ps. 10:7]. 'Their feet are swift to shed blood; in their paths are ruin and misery' [Isa. 59:7 p]. There is no fear of God before their eyes" [Rom. 3:10–16, 18 p]. With these thunderbolts he inveighs not against particular men but against the whole race of Adam's children. Nor is he decrying the depraved morals of one age or another, but indicting the unvarying corruption of our nature. Now his intention in this passage is not simply to rebuke men that they may repent, but rather to teach them that they have all been overwhelmed by an unavoidable calamity from which only God's mercy can deliver them.

II.iii.3   Almost the same question that was previously answered now confronts us anew. In every age there have been persons who, guided by nature, have striven toward virtue throughout life. I have nothing to say against them even if many lapses can be noted in their moral conduct. For they have by the very zeal of their honesty given proof that there was some purity in their nature. . . . These examples, accordingly, seem to warn us against adjudging man's nature wholly corrupted, because some men have by its prompting not only excelled in remarkable deeds, but conducted themselves most honorably throughout life. But here it ought to occur to us that amid this corruption of nature there is some place for God's grace; not such grace as to cleanse it, but to restrain it inwardly. For if the Lord gave loose rein to the mind of each man to run riot in his lusts, there would doubtless be no one who would not show that, in fact, every evil thing for which Paul condemns all nature is most truly to be met in himself [Ps. 14:3; Rom. 3:12].

What then? Do you count yourself exempt from the number of those whose "feet are swift to shed blood" [Rom. 3:15], whose hands are fouled with robberies and murders, "whose throats are like open graves, whose tongues deceive, whose lips are envenomed" [Rom. 3:13]; whose works are useless, wicked, rotten, deadly; whose hearts are without God; whose inmost parts, depravities; whose eyes are set upon stratagems; whose minds are eager to revile—to sum up, whose every part stands ready to commit infinite wickedness [Rom. 3:10–18]? If every soul is subject to such abominations as the apostle boldly declares, we surely see what would happen if the Lord were to permit human lust to wander according to its own inclination. . . . Thus God by his providence bridles perversity of nature, that it may not break forth into action; but he does not purge it within.

II.iii.5   Man, as he was corrupted by the Fall, sinned willingly, not unwillingly or by compulsion; by the most eager inclination of his heart, not by forced compulsion; by the prompting of his own lust, not by compulsion from without. Yet so depraved is his nature that he can be moved or impelled only to evil. But if this is true, then it is clearly expressed that man is surely subject to the necessity of sinning.

3. HUMAN GOOD IS DUE TO THE GRACE OF GOD

II.iii.6   On the other hand, it behooves us to consider the sort of remedy by which divine grace corrects and cures the corruption of nature. Since the Lord in coming to our aid bestows upon us what we lack, when the nature of his work in us appears, our destitution will, on the other hand, at once be manifest. When the apostle tells the Philippians he is confident "that he who began a good work in you will bring it to completion at the day of Jesus Christ" [Phil. 1:6], there is no doubt that through "the beginning of a good work" he denotes the very origin of conversion itself, which is in the will. God begins his good work in us, therefore, by arousing love and desire and zeal for righteousness in our hearts; or, to speak more correctly, by bending, forming, and directing, our hearts to righteousness. He completes his work, moreover, by confirming us to perseverance. . . .

If in a stone there is such plasticity that, made softer by some means, it becomes somewhat bent, I will not deny that man's heart can be molded to obey the right, provided what is imperfect in him be supplied by God's grace. But if by this comparison the Lord wished to show that nothing good can ever be wrung from our heart, unless it become wholly other, let us not divide between him and us what he claims for himself alone. If, therefore, a stone is transformed into flesh when God converts us to zeal for the right, whatever is of our own will is effaced. What takes its place is wholly from God. I say that the will is effaced; not in so far as it is will, for in man's conversion what belongs to his primal nature remains entire. I also say that it is created anew; not meaning that the will now begins to exist, but that it is changed from an evil to a good will. . . . Everything good in the will is the work of grace alone.

II.iii.7   But perhaps some will concede that the will is turned away from the good by its own nature and is converted by the Lord's power alone, yet in such a way that, having been prepared, it then has its own part in the action. As Augustine teaches, grace precedes every good work; while will does not go before as its leader but follows after as its attendant. . . . In so far as it is anticipated by grace, to that degree I concede that you may call your will an "attendant." But because the will reformed is the Lord's work, it is wrongly attributed to man that he obeys prevenient grace with his will as attendant. . . . Nor was it Augustine's intent, in calling the human will the attendant of grace, to assign to the will in good works a function second to that of grace. His only purpose was, rather, to refute that very evil doctrine of Pelagius which lodged the first cause of salvation in man's merit. Enough for the argument at hand, Augustine contends, was the fact that grace is prior to all merit.

II.iii.8   Surely there is ready and sufficient reason to believe that good takes its origin from God alone. And only in the elect does one find a will inclined to good. Yet we must seek the cause of election outside men. It follows, thence, that man has a right will not from himself, but that it flows from the same good pleasure by which we were chosen before the creation of the world [Eph. 1:4].

II.iii.11   Perseverance would, without any doubt, be accounted God's free gift if a most wicked error did not prevail that it is distributed according to men's merit, in so far as each man shows himself receptive to the first grace. But since this error arose from the fact that men thought it in their power to spurn or to accept the proffered grace of God, when the latter opinion is swept away the former idea also falls of itself. . . . But here we ought to guard against two things: (1) not to say that lawful use of the first grace is rewarded by later graces, as if man by his own effort rendered God's grace effective; or (2) so to think of the reward as to cease to consider it of God's free grace. I grant that believers are to expect this blessing of God: that the better use they have made of the prior graces, the more may the following graces be thereafter increased. But I say this use is also from the Lord and this reward arises from his free benevolence.

XII

SIN AND THE LAW OF GOD

1. HUMAN INABILITY TO KEEP THE LAW

II.vi.1 The whole human race perished in the person of Adam. Consequently that original excellence and nobility which we have recounted would be of no profit to us but would rather redound to our greater shame, until God, who does not recognize as his handiwork men defiled and corrupted by sin, appeared as Redeemer in the person of his only-begotten Son. Therefore, since we have fallen from life into death, the whole knowledge of God the Creator that we have discussed would be useless unless faith also followed, setting forth for us God our Father in Christ. . . .

For even if God wills to manifest his fatherly favor to us in many ways, yet we cannot by contemplating the universe infer that he is Father. Rather, conscience presses us within and shows in our sin just cause for his disowning us and not regarding or recognizing us as his sons. Dullness and ingratitude follow, for our minds, as they have been blinded, do not perceive what is true. And as all our senses have become perverted, we wickedly defraud God of his glory.

We must, for this reason, come to Paul's statement: "Since in the wisdom of God the world did not know God through wisdom, it pleased God through the folly of preaching to save those who believe" [1 Cor. 1:21]. This magnificent theater of heaven and earth, crammed with innumerable miracles, Paul calls the "wisdom of God." Contemplating it, we ought in wisdom to have known God. But because we have profited so little by it, he calls us to the faith of Christ, which, because it appears foolish, the unbelievers despise.

Therefore, although the preaching of the cross does not agree with our human inclination, if we desire to return to God our Author and Maker, from whom we have been estranged, in order that he may again begin to be our Father, we ought nevertheless to embrace it humbly. Surely, after the fall of the first man no knowledge of God apart from the Mediator has had power unto salvation [cf. Rom. 1:16; 1 Cor. 1:24]. For Christ not only speaks of his own age, but comprehends all ages when he says: "This is eternal life, to know the Father to be the one true God, and Jesus Christ whom he has sent" [John 17:3 p].

II.vi.4   Apart from Christ the saving knowledge of God does not stand. From the beginning of the world he had consequently been set before all the elect that they should look unto him and put their trust in him.

II.vii.8   The wickedness and condemnation of us all are sealed by the testimony of the law. Yet this is not done to cause us to fall down in despair or, completely discouraged, to rush headlong over the brink—provided we duly profit by the testimony of the law. It is true that in this way the wicked are terrified, but because of their obstinacy of heart. For the children of God the knowledge of the law should have another purpose. The apostle testifies that we are indeed condemned by the judgment of the law, "so that every mouth may be stopped, and the whole world may be held accountable to God" [Rom. 3:19]. He teaches the same idea in yet another place: "For God has shut up all men in unbelief," not that he may destroy all or suffer all to perish, but "that he may have mercy upon all" [Rom. 11:32]. This means that, dismissing the stupid opinion of their own strength, they come to realize that they stand and are upheld by God's hand alone; that, naked and empty-handed, they flee to his mercy, repose entirely in it, hide deep within it, and seize upon it alone for righteousness and merit. For God's mercy is revealed in Christ to all who seek and wait upon it with true faith. In the precepts of the law, God is but the rewarder of perfect righteousness, which all of us lack, and conversely, the severe judge of evil deeds. But in Christ his face shines, full of grace and gentleness, even upon us poor and unworthy sinners.

2. THE TEN COMMANDMENTS

II.viii.1   Here I think it will not be out of place to introduce the Ten Commandments of the law with a short explanation of them. Thus, the point I have touched upon will also be made clearer: that the public worship that God once prescribed is still in force. Then will come the confirmation of my second point: that the Jews not only learned from the law what the true character of godliness was; but also that, since they saw themselves incapable of observing the law, they were in dread of judgment drawn inevitably though unwillingly to the Mediator. Now in summarizing what is required for the true knowledge of God, we have taught that we cannot conceive him in his greatness without being immediately confronted by his majesty, and so compelled to worship him. In our discussion of the knowledge of ourselves we have set forth this chief point: that, empty of all opinion of our own virtue, and shorn of all assurance of our own righteousness—in fact, broken and crushed by the awareness of our own utter poverty—we may learn genuine humility and self-abasement. Both of these the Lord accomplishes in his law. First, claiming for himself the lawful power to command, he calls us to reverence his divinity, and specifies wherein such reverence lies and consists. Secondly, having published the rule of his righteousness, he reproves us both for our impotence and for our unrighteousness. For our nature, wicked and deformed, is always opposing his uprightness; and our capacity, weak and feeble to do good, lies far from his perfection.

Now that inward law, which we have above described as written, even engraved, upon the hearts of all, in a sense asserts the very same things that are to be learned from the two Tables. For our conscience does not allow us to sleep a perpetual insensible sleep without being an inner witness and monitor of what we owe God, without holding before us the difference between good and evil and thus accusing us when we fail in our duty. But man is so shrouded in the darkness of errors that he hardly begins to grasp through this natural law what worship is acceptable to God. Surely he is very far removed from a true estimate of it. Besides this, he is so puffed up with haughtiness and ambition, and so blinded by self-love, that he is as yet unable to look upon himself and, as it were, to descend within himself, that he may humble and abase himself and confess his own miserable condition. Accordingly (because it is necessary both for our dullness and for our arrogance), the Lord has provided us with a written law to give us a clearer witness of what was too obscure in the natural law, shake off our listlessness, and strike more vigorously our mind and memory.

The First Commandment

II.viii.13   "I am Jehovah, your God, who brought you out of the
             land of Egypt, out of the house of bondage. You shall
have no other gods before my face" [Ex. 20:2–3; cf. Vg.].

Whether you make the first sentence a part of the First
Commandment or read it separately makes no difference to
me, provided you do not deny to me that it is a sort of preface
to the whole law.

II.viii.14   God first shows himself to be the one who has the
             right to command and to whom obedience is due.

II.viii.16   Having founded and established the authority of his
             law, he sets forth the First Commandment, "Let us
have no strange gods before him" [Ex. 20:3 p]. The purpose of
this commandment is that the Lord wills alone to be pre-
eminent among his people, and to exercise complete authority
over them. To effect this, he enjoins us to put far from us all
impiety and superstition, which either diminish or obscure the
glory of his divinity. For the same reason he commands us to
worship and adore him with true and zealous godliness. The
very simplicity of the words well-nigh expresses this. For we
cannot "have" God without at the same time embracing the
things that are his. Therefore, in forbidding us to have strange
gods, he means that we are not to transfer to another what
belongs to him.

The Second Commandment

II.viii.17   "You shall not make yourself a graven image, or any
             likeness of anything that is in heaven above, or in the
earth beneath, or in the waters which are under the earth; you
shall not adore or worship them" [Ex. 20:4–5; cf. Vg.]. . . .

The purpose of this commandment, then, is that he does not
will that his lawful worship be profaned by superstitious rites.
To sum up, he wholly calls us back and withdraws us from
petty carnal observances, which our stupid minds, crassly con-
ceiving of God, are wont to devise. And then he makes us
conform to his lawful worship, that is, a spiritual worship established by himself. Moreover, he marks the grossest fault in this
transgression, outward idolatry.

The Third Commandment

II.viii.22 "You shall not take the name of Jehovah your God in vain" [Ex. 20:7].

The purpose of this commandment is: God wills that we hallow the majesty of his name. Therefore, it means in brief that we are not to profane his name by treating it contemptuously and irreverently. To this prohibition duly corresponds the commandment that we should be zealous and careful to honor his name with godly reverence. Therefore we ought to be so disposed in mind and speech that we neither think nor say anything concerning God and his mysteries, without reverence and much soberness; that in estimating his works we conceive nothing but what is honorable to him.

The Fourth Commandment

II.viii.28 "Remember to keep holy the Sabbath Day. Six days you shall labor, and do all your work; but the seventh day is a sabbath to Jehovah your God. In it you shall not do any work," etc. [Ex. 20:8–10; cf. Vg.].

The purpose of this commandment is that, being dead to our own inclinations and works, we should meditate on the Kingdom of God, and that we should practice that meditation in the ways established by him. But, since this commandment has a particular consideration distinct from the others, it requires a slightly different order of exposition. The early fathers customarily called this commandment a foreshadowing because it contains the outward keeping of a day which, upon Christ's coming, was abolished with the other figures. This they say truly, but they touch upon only half the matter. Hence, we must go deeper in our exposition, and ponder three conditions in which, it seems to me, the keeping of this commandment consists.

First, under the repose of the seventh day the heavenly Lawgiver meant to represent to the people of Israel spiritual rest, in which believers ought to lay aside their own works to allow God to work in them. Secondly, he meant that there was to be a stated day for them to assemble to hear the law and perform the rites, or at least to devote it particularly to meditation upon his works, and thus through this remembrance to be trained in piety. Thirdly, he resolved to give a day of rest to servants and those who are under the authority of others, in order that they should have some respite from toil.

The Fifth Commandment

II.viii.35   "Honor your father and your mother that you may be
long-lived on the land which Jehovah your God shall
give you" [Ex. 20:12; cf. Vg.].

The purpose is: since the maintenance of his economy
pleases the Lord God, the degrees of pre-eminence established
by him ought to be inviolable for us. This, then, is the sum: that
we should look up to those whom God has placed over us, and
should treat them with honor, obedience, and gratefulness.

II.viii.36   For this reason, we ought not to doubt that the Lord
has here established a universal rule. That is, knowing
that someone has been placed over us by the Lord's ordination,
we should render to him reverence, obedience, and gratefulness, and should perform such other duties for him as we can.
It makes no difference whether our superiors are worthy or
unworthy of this honor, for whatever they are they have attained their position through God's providence—a proof that
the Lawgiver himself would have us hold them in honor. However, he has expressly bidden us to reverence our parents, who
have brought us into this life. Nature itself ought in a way to
teach us this.

The Sixth Commandment

II.viii.39   "You shall not kill" [Ex. 20:13, Vg.].

The purpose of this commandment is: the Lord has
bound mankind together by a certain unity; hence each man
ought to concern himself with the safety of all. To sum up,
then, all violence, injury, and any harmful thing at all that may
injure our neighbor's body are forbidden to us. We are accordingly commanded, if we find anything of use to us in saving our
neighbors' lives, faithfully to employ it; if there is anything that
makes for their peace, to see to it; if anything harmful, to ward
it off; if they are in any danger, to lend a helping hand. If you
recall that God is so speaking as Lawgiver, ponder at the same
time that by this rule he wills to guide your soul. For it would
be ridiculous that he who looks upon the thoughts of the heart
and dwells especially upon them, should instruct only the body
in true righteousness. Therefore this law also forbids murder
of the heart, and enjoins the inner intent to save a brother's
life.

The Seventh Commandment

II.viii.41 "You shall not commit adultery" [Ex. 20:14, Vg.].

The purpose of this commandment is: because God loves modesty and purity, all uncleanness must be far from us. To sum up, then: we should not become defiled with any filth or lustful intemperance of the flesh. To this corresponds the affirmative commandment that we chastely and continently regulate all parts of our life. But he expressly forbids fornication, to which all lust tends, in order through the foulness of fornication, which is grosser and more palpable, in so far as it brands the body also with its mark, to lead us to abominate all lust.

II.viii.44 Now if married couples recognize that their association is blessed by the Lord, they are thereby admonished not to pollute it with uncontrolled and dissolute lust. For even if the honorableness of matrimony covers the baseness of incontinence, it ought not for that reason to be a provocation thereto. Therefore let not married persons think that all things are permitted to them, but let each man have his own wife soberly, and each wife her own husband. So doing, let them not admit anything at all that is unworthy of the honorableness and temperance of marriage. For it is fitting that thus wedlock contracted in the Lord be recalled to measure and modesty so as not to wallow in extreme lewdness. . . .

And lest there be any doubt, remember that God is here commending modesty. If the Lord requires modesty of us, he condemns whatever opposes it. Consequently, if you aspire to obedience, let neither your heart burn with wicked lust within, nor your eyes wantonly run into corrupt desires, nor your body be decked with bawdy ornaments, nor your tongue seduce your mind to like thoughts with filthy words, nor your appetite inflame it with intemperance. For all vices of this sort are like blemishes, which besmirch the purity of chastity.

The Eighth Commandment

II.viii.45 "You shall not steal" [Ex. 20:15, Vg.].

The purpose of this commandment is: since injustice is an abomination to God, we should render to each man what belongs to him [Rom. 13:7]. To sum up: we are forbidden to pant after the possessions of others, and consequently are commanded to strive faithfully to help every man to keep his own possessions. . . .

Now there are many kinds of thefts. One consists in violence, when another's goods are stolen by force and unrestrained brigandage. A second kind consists in malicious deceit, when they are carried off through fraud. Another lies in a more concealed craftiness, when a man's goods are snatched from him by seemingly legal means. Still another lies in flatteries, when one is cheated of his goods under the pretense of a gift.

II.viii.46   We will duly obey this commandment, then, if, content with our lot, we are zealous to make only honest and lawful gain; if we do not seek to become wealthy through injustice, nor attempt to deprive our neighbor of his goods to increase our own; if we do not strive to heap up riches cruelly wrung from the blood of others; if we do not madly scrape together from everywhere, by fair means or foul, whatever will feed our avarice or satisfy our prodigality. On the other hand, let this be our constant aim: faithfully to help all men by our counsel and aid to keep what is theirs, in so far as we can; but if we have to deal with faithless and deceitful men, let us be prepared to give up something of our own rather than to contend with them. And not this alone: but let us share the necessity of those whom we see pressed by the difficulty of affairs, assisting them in their need with our abundance.

The Ninth Commandment

II.viii.47   "You shall not be a false witness against your neighbor" [Ex. 20:16].

The purpose of this commandment is: since God (who is truth) abhors a lie, we must practice truth without deceit toward one another. To sum up, then: let us not malign anyone with slanders or false charges, nor harm his substance by falsehood, in short, injure him by unbridled evilspeaking and impudence. To this prohibition the command is linked that we should faithfully help everyone as much as we can in affirming the truth, in order to protect the integrity of his name and possessions. . . .

Hence this commandment is lawfully observed when our tongue, in declaring the truth, serves both the good repute and the advantage of our neighbors. The equity of this is quite evident. For if a good name is more precious than all riches [Prov. 22:1], we harm a man more by despoiling him of the integrity of his name than by taking away his possessions. In plundering his substance, however, we sometimes do as much by false testimony as by snatching with our hands.

The Tenth Commandment

II.viii.49   "You shall not covet your neighbor's house," etc. [Ex. 20:17, Vg.].

The purpose of this commandment is: since God wills that our whole soul be possessed with a disposition to love, we must banish from our hearts all desire contrary to love. To sum up, then: no thought should steal upon us to move our hearts to a harmful covetousness that tends to our neighbor's loss. To this corresponds the opposite precept: whatever we conceive, deliberate, will, or attempt is to be linked to our neighbor's good and advantage. . . . The Lord has previously commanded that the rule of love govern our wills, our endeavors, and our actions. Now he enjoins that the thoughts of our mind be so controlled to the same end that none of them may become depraved or twisted and thus drive the mind in the opposite direction. As he has forbidden our minds to be inclined and led into anger, hatred, adultery, robbery, and lying, he now prohibits them from being prompted thereto.

II.viii.51   Now it will not be difficult to decide the purpose of the whole law: the fulfillment of righteousness to form human life to the archetype of divine purity. For God has so depicted his character in the law that if any man carries out in deeds whatever is enjoined there, he will express the image of God, as it were, in his own life. For this reason, Moses, wishing to remind the Israelites of the gist of the law, said: "And now, Israel, what does the Lord your God require of you, but to fear the Lord . . . , to walk in his ways, to love him, to serve him with all your heart and with all your soul, and to keep his commandments?" [Deut. 10:12–13; cf. Vg.]. And Moses did not cease to harp on this same thought to them whenever he had to point out the aim of the law. Here is the object of the teaching of the law: to join man by holiness of life to his God, and, as Moses elsewhere says, to make him cleave to God [cf. Deut. 11:22 or 30:20].

XIII

THE PERSON OF CHRIST

1. THE MEDIATOR

II.xii.1   Now it was of the greatest importance for us that he who was to be our Mediator be both true God and true man.... Since our iniquities, like a cloud cast between us and him, had completely estranged us from the Kingdom of Heaven [cf. Isa. 59:2], no man, unless he belonged to God, could serve as the intermediary to restore peace. But who might reach to him? Any one of Adam's children? ... The situation would surely have been hopeless had the very majesty of God not descended to us, since it was not in our power to ascend to him. Hence, it was necessary for the Son of God to become for us "Immanuel, that is, God with us" [Isa. 7:14; Matt. 1:23], and in such a way that his divinity and our human nature might by mutual connection grow together. Otherwise the nearness would not have been near enough, nor the affinity sufficiently firm, for us to hope that God might dwell with us. So great was the disagreement between our uncleanness and God's perfect purity!

II.xii.2   What the Mediator was to accomplish was no common thing. His task was so to restore us to God's grace as to make of the children of men, children of God; of the heirs of Gehenna, heirs of the Heavenly Kingdom. Who could have done this had not the selfsame Son of God become the Son of man, and had not so taken what was ours as to impart what was his to us, and to make what was his by nature ours by grace? ...

For the same reason it was also imperative that he who was to become our Redeemer be true God and true man. It was his task to swallow up death. Who but the Life could do this? It was his task to conquer sin. Who but very Righteousness could do this? It was his task to rout the powers of world and air. Who but a power higher than world and air could do this? Now where does life or righteousness, or lordship and authority of heaven lie but with God alone? Therefore our most merciful God, when he willed that we be redeemed, made himself our Redeemer in the person of his only-begotten Son [cf. Rom. 5:8].

II.xii.3   Clothed with our flesh he vanquished death and sin together that the victory and triumph might be ours. He offered as a sacrifice the flesh he received from us, that he might wipe out our guilt by his act of expiation and appease the Father's righteous wrath.

II.xii.4   He who ponders these matters with the diligent attention they require will readily have done with the vague speculations that captivate the frivolous and the seekers after novelty. One such speculation is that Christ would still have become man even if no means of redeeming mankind had been needed. . . . We well know why Christ was promised from the beginning: to restore the fallen world and to succor lost men. . . . The only reason given in Scripture that the Son of God willed to take our flesh, and accepted this commandment from the Father, is that he would be a sacrifice to appease the Father on our behalf.

2. THE TWO NATURES OF CHRIST

II.xiv.1   We ought not to understand the statement that "the Word was made flesh" [John 1:14] in the sense that the Word was turned into flesh or confusedly mingled with flesh. Rather, it means that, because he chose for himself the virgin's womb as a temple in which to dwell, he who was the Son of God became the Son of man—not by confusion of substance, but by unity of person. For we affirm his divinity so joined and united with his humanity that each retains its distinctive nature unimpaired, and yet these two natures constitute one Christ.

If anything like this very great mystery can be found in human affairs, the most apposite parallel seems to be that of man, whom we see to consist of two substances. Yet neither is so mingled with the other as not to retain its own distinctive nature. For the soul is not the body, and the body is not the soul. Therefore, some things are said exclusively of the soul that can in no wise apply to the body; and of the body, again, that in no way fit the soul; of the whole man, that cannot refer—except inappropriately—to either soul or body separately. Finally, the characteristics of the mind are [sometimes] transferred to the body, and those of the body to the soul. Yet he who consists of these parts is one man, not many. Such expressions signify both that there is one person in man composed of two elements joined together, and that there are two diverse underlying natures that make up this person. Thus, also, the Scriptures speak of Christ: they sometimes attribute to him what must be referred solely to his humanity, sometimes what belongs uniquely to his divinity; and sometimes what embraces both natures but fits neither alone. And they so earnestly express this union of the two natures that is in Christ as sometimes to interchange them. This figure of speech is called by the ancient writers "the communicating of properties."

II.xiv.3   The passages that comprehend both natures at once, very many of which are to be found in John's Gospel, set forth his true substance most clearly of all. For one reads there neither of deity nor of humanity alone, but of both at once: he received from the Father the power of remitting sins [John 1:29], of raising to life whom he will, of bestowing righteousness, holiness, salvation; he was appointed judge of the living and the dead in order that he might be honored, even as the Father [John 5:21–23]. Lastly, he is called the "light of the world" [John 8:12; 9:5], the "good shepherd," the "only door" [John 10:11, 9], the "true vine" [John 15:1].

II.xiv.4   It is amazing how much untutored minds—and even some not completely uneducated—are plagued by expressions of this sort, which they see applied to Christ, yet not quite appropriate either to his divinity or to his humanity. This is because they do not consider the expressions suitable either to his person, in which he was manifested as God and man, or to the office of the Mediator.

XIV

THE WORK OF CHRIST

1. THE THREEFOLD OFFICE

II.xv.1   That faith may find a firm basis for salvation in Christ, and thus rest in him, this principle must be laid down: the office enjoined upon Christ by the Father consists of three parts. For he was given to be prophet, king, and priest. Yet it would be of little value to know these names without understanding their purpose and use.

II.xv.2   Now it is to be noted that the title "Christ" pertains to these three offices: for we know that under the law prophets as well as priests and kings were anointed with holy oil. Hence the illustrious name of "Messiah" was also bestowed upon the promised Mediator. As I have elsewhere shown, I recognize that Christ was called Messiah especially with respect to, and by virtue of, his kingship. Yet his anointings as prophet and as priest have their place and must not be overlooked by us. Isaiah specifically mentions the former in these words: "The Spirit of the Lord Jehovah is upon me, because Jehovah has anointed me to preach to the humble, . . . to bring healing to the brokenhearted, to proclaim liberation to the captives . . . , to proclaim the year of the Lord's good pleasure," etc. [Isa. 61:1–2; cf. Luke 4:18]. We see that he was anointed by the Spirit to be herald and witness of the Father's grace. And that not in the common way—for he is distinguished from other teachers with a similar office. . . .The prophetic dignity in Christ leads us to know that in the sum of doctrine as he has given it to us all parts of perfect wisdom are contained.

II.xv.3   I come now to kingship. It would be pointless to speak of this without first warning my readers that it is spiritual in nature. . . . Speaking in the person of God, David says: "Sit at my right hand, till I make your enemies your footstool" [Ps. 110:1]. Here he asserts that, no matter how many strong enemies plot to overthrow the church, they do not have sufficient strength to prevail over God's immutable decree by which he appointed his Son eternal King. Hence it follows that the devil, with all the resources of the world, can never destroy the church, founded as it is on the eternal throne of Christ. Now with regard to the special application of this to each one of us—the same "eternity" ought to inspire us to hope for blessed immortality.

II.xv.4   Thus it is that we may patiently pass through this life with its misery, hunger, cold, contempt, reproaches, and other troubles—content with this one thing: that our King will never leave us destitute, but will provide for our needs until, our warfare ended, we are called to triumph. Such is the nature of his rule, that he shares with us all that he has received from the Father. Now he arms and equips us with his power, adorns us with his beauty and magnificence, enriches us with his wealth. These benefits, then, give us the most fruitful occasion to glory, and also provide us with confidence to struggle fearlessly against the devil, sin, and death. Finally, clothed with his righteousness, we can valiantly rise above all the world's reproaches; and just as he himself freely lavishes his gifts upon us, so may we, in return, bring forth fruit to his glory.

II.xv.6   Now we must speak briefly concerning the purpose and use of Christ's priestly office: as a pure and stainless Mediator he is by his holiness to reconcile us to God. But God's righteous curse bars our access to him, and God in his capacity as judge is angry toward us. Hence, an expiation must intervene in order that Christ as priest may obtain God's favor for us and appease his wrath. Thus Christ to perform this office had to come forward with a sacrifice. . . . The priestly office belongs to Christ alone because by the sacrifice of his death he blotted out our own guilt and made satisfaction for our sins [Heb. 9:22]. . . .

It follows that he is an everlasting intercessor: through his pleading we obtain favor. Hence arises not only trust in prayer, but also peace for godly consciences, while they safely lean upon God's fatherly mercy and are surely persuaded that whatever has been consecrated through the Mediator is pleasing to God. . . .

Christ plays the priestly role, not only to render the Father favorable and propitious toward us by an eternal law of reconciliation, but also to receive us as his companions in this great office [Rev. 1:6]. For we who are defiled in ourselves, yet are priests in him, offer ourselves and our all to God, and freely enter the heavenly sanctuary that the sacrifices of prayers and praise that we bring may be acceptable and sweet-smelling before God.

2. THE DEATH, RESURRECTION, AND ASCENSION OF CHRIST

II.xvi.1 What we have said so far concerning Christ must be referred to this one objective: condemned, dead, and lost in ourselves, we should seek righteousness, liberation, life, and salvation in him. . . . But here we must earnestly ponder how he accomplishes salvation for us. This we must do not only to be persuaded that he is its author, but to gain a sufficient and stable support for our faith, rejecting whatever could draw us away in one direction or another.

II.xvi.2 But, before we go any farther, we must see in passing how fitting it was that God, who anticipates us by his mercy, should have been our enemy until he was reconciled to us through Christ. For how could he have given in his only-begotten Son a singular pledge of his love to us if he had not already embraced us with his free favor?

II.xvi.3 God, who is the highest righteousness, cannot love the unrighteousness that he sees in us all. All of us, therefore, have in ourselves something deserving of God's hatred. With regard to our corrupt nature and the wicked life that follows it, all of us surely displease God, are guilty in his sight, and are born to the damnation of hell. But because the Lord wills not to lose what is his in us, out of his own kindness he still finds something to love. However much we may be sinners by our own fault, we nevertheless remain his creatures. However much we have brought death upon ourselves, yet he has created us unto life. Thus he is moved by pure and freely given love of us to receive us into grace. Since there is a perpetual and irreconcilable disagreement between righteousness and unrighteousness, so long as we remain sinners he cannot receive us completely. Therefore, to take away all cause for enmity and to reconcile us utterly to himself, he wipes out all evil in us by the expiation set forth in the death of Christ; that we, who were previously unclean and impure, may show ourselves righteous and holy in his sight. Therefore, by his love God the Father goes before and anticipates our reconciliation in Christ. Indeed, "because he first loved us" [1 John 4:19], he afterward reconciles us to himself. But until Christ succors us by his death, the unrighteousness that deserves God's indignation remains in us, and is accursed and condemned before him. Hence, we can be fully and firmly joined with God only when Christ joins us with him. If, then, we would be assured that God is pleased with and kindly disposed toward us, we must fix our eyes and minds on Christ alone. For actually, through him alone we escape the imputation of our sins to us—an imputation bringing with it the wrath of God.

II.xvi.5   Now someone asks, How has Christ abolished sin, banished the separation between us and God, and acquired righteousness to render God favorable and kindly toward us? To this we can in general reply that he has achieved this for us by the whole course of his obedience. This is proved by Paul's testimony: "As by one man's disobedience many were made sinners, so by one man's obedience we are made righteous" [Rom. 5:19 p]. . . .

The so-called "Apostles' Creed" passes at once in the best order from the birth of Christ to his death and resurrection, wherein the whole of perfect salvation consists. Yet the remainder of the obedience that he manifested in his life is not excluded. Paul embraces it all from beginning to end: "He emptied himself, taking the form of a servant, . . . and was obedient to the Father unto death, even death on a cross" [Phil. 2:7–8 p]. And truly, even in death itself his willing obedience is the important thing because a sacrifice not offered voluntarily would not have furthered righteousness. . . . This is our acquittal: the guilt that held us liable for punishment has been transferred to the head of the Son of God [Isa. 53:12]. We must, above all, remember this substitution, lest we tremble and remain anxious throughout life—as if God's righteous vengeance, which the Son of God has taken upon himself, still hung over us.

II.xvi.7   There follows in the Creed: "He was dead and buried." Here again is to be seen how he in every respect took our place to pay the price of our redemption. Death held us captive under its yoke; Christ, in our stead, gave himself over to its power to deliver us from it. So the apostle understands it when he writes: "He tasted death for everyone" [Heb.

2:9 p]. By dying, he ensured that we would not die, or—which is the same thing—redeemed us to life by his own death. He differed from us, however, in this respect: he let himself be swallowed up by death, as it were, not to be engulfed in its abyss, but rather to engulf it [cf. 1 Peter 3:22, Vg.] that must soon have engulfed us; he let himself be subjected to it, not to be overwhelmed by its power, but rather to lay it low, when it was threatening us and exulting over our fallen state.

II.xvi.13   Next comes the resurrection from the dead. Without this what we have said so far would be incomplete. For since only weakness appears in the cross, death, and burial of Christ, faith must leap over all these things to attain its full strength. We have in his death the complete fulfillment of salvation, for through it we are reconciled to God, his righteous judgment is satisfied, the curse is removed, and the penalty paid in full. Nevertheless, we are said to "have been born anew to a living hope" not through his death but "through his resurrection" [1 Peter 1:3 p]. For as he, in rising again, came forth victor over death, so the victory of our faith over death lies in his resurrection alone. Paul's words better express its nature: "He was put to death for our sins, and raised for our justification" [Rom. 4:25]. This is as if he had said: "Sin was taken away by his death; righteousness was revived and restored by his resurrection." For how could he by dying have freed us from death if he had himself succumbed to death? How could he have acquired victory for us if he had failed in the struggle? Therefore, we divide the substance of our salvation between Christ's death and resurrection as follows: through his death, sin was wiped out and death extinguished; through his resurrection, righteousness was restored and life raised up, so that— thanks to his resurrection—his death manifested its power and efficacy in us.

II.xvi.14   To the resurrection is quite appropriately joined the ascent into heaven. Now having laid aside the mean and lowly state of mortal life and the shame of the cross, Christ by rising again began to show forth his glory and power more fully. Yet he truly inaugurated his Kingdom only at his ascension into heaven.

II.xvi.18   Hence arises a wonderful consolation: that we perceive judgment to be in the hands of him who has already destined us to share with him the honor of judging [cf. Matt. 19:28]! Far indeed is he from mounting his judgment seat

to condemn us! How could our most merciful Ruler destroy his
people? How could the Head scatter his own members? How
could our Advocate condemn his clients? For if the apostle
dares exclaim that with Christ interceding for us there is no
one who can come forth to condemn us [Rom. 8:34, 33], it is
much more true, then, that Christ as Intercessor will not condemn those whom he has received into his charge and protection. No mean assurance, this—that we shall be brought before
no other judgment seat than that of our Redeemer, to whom
we must look for our salvation! Moreover, he who now promises eternal blessedness through the gospel will then fulfill his
promise in judgment. Therefore, by giving all judgment to the
Son [John 5:22], the Father has honored him to the end that
he may care for the consciences of his people, who tremble in
dread of judgment.

II.xvi.19   We see that our whole salvation and all its parts are
comprehended in Christ [Acts 4:12]. We should therefore take care not to derive the least portion of it from any-
where else. If we seek salvation, we are taught by the very
name of Jesus that it is "of him" [1 Cor. 1:30]. If we seek any
other gifts of the Spirit, they will be found in his anointing. If
we seek strength, it lies in his dominion; if purity, in his conception; if gentleness, it appears in his birth. For by his birth
he was made like us in all respects [Heb. 2:17] that he might
learn to feel our pain [cf. Heb. 5:2]. If we seek redemption, it
lies in his passion; if acquittal, in his condemnation; if remission
of the curse, in his cross [Gal. 3:13]; if satisfaction, in his sacrifice; if purification, in his blood; if reconciliation, in his descent
into hell; if mortification of the flesh, in his tomb; if newness
of life, in his resurrection; if immortality, in the same; if inheritance of the Heavenly Kingdom, in his entrance into heaven;
if protection, if security, if abundant supply of all blessings, in
his Kingdom; if untroubled expectation of judgment, in the
power given to him to judge. In short, since rich store of every
kind of good abounds in him, let us drink our fill from this
fountain, and from no other.

BOOK THREE

THE HOLY SPIRIT

XV

THE WORK
OF THE HOLY SPIRIT

1. SALVATION

III.i.1   We must now examine this question. How do we receive those benefits which the Father bestowed on his only-begotten Son—not for Christ's own private use, but that he might enrich poor and needy men? First, we must understand that as long as Christ remains outside of us, and we are separated from him, all that he has suffered and done for the salvation of the human race remains useless and of no value for us. Therefore, to share with us what he has received from the Father, he had to become ours and to dwell within us. . . . It is true that we obtain this by faith. Yet since we see that not all indiscriminately embrace that communion with Christ which is offered through the gospel, reason itself teaches us to climb higher and to examine into the secret energy of the Spirit, by which we come to enjoy Christ and all his benefits. . . . The Holy Spirit is the bond by which Christ effectually unites us to himself.

III.i.2   We must bear in mind that Christ came endowed with the Holy Spirit in a special way: that is, to separate us from the world and to gather us unto the hope of the eternal inheritance. . . . To the Kingdom of Christ, then, the prophets give the lofty title of the time when there will be a richer outpouring of the Spirit. There is a passage in Joel notable above all others: "And in that day I shall pour forth of my spirit upon all flesh" [ch. 2:28 p]. For even if the prophet seems to restrict the gifts of the Spirit to the prophetic office, under this figure he signifies that, in manifesting his Spirit, God will make disciples of those who were previously destitute and empty of heavenly doctrine. Further, God the Father gives us the Holy Spirit for his Son's sake, and yet has bestowed the whole fullness of the Spirit upon the Son to be minister and steward of his liberality. For this reason, the Spirit is sometimes called the "Spirit of the Father," sometimes the "Spirit of the Son."

III.i.3   It is useful to note what titles are applied to the Holy Spirit in Scripture, when the beginning and the whole renewal of our salvation are under discussion. First, he is called the "spirit of adoption" because he is the witness to us of the free benevolence of God with which God the Father has embraced us in his beloved only-begotten Son to become a Father to us; and he encourages us to have trust in prayer. In fact, he supplies the very words so that we may fearlessly cry, "Abba, Father!" [Rom. 8:15; Gal. 4:6]. For the same reason he is called "the guarantee and seal" of our inheritance [2 Cor. 1:22; cf. Eph. 1:14] because from heaven he so gives life to us, on pilgrimage in the world and resembling dead men, as to assure us that our salvation is safe in God's unfailing care. He is also called "life" because of righteousness [cf. Rom. 8:10].

By his secret watering the Spirit makes us fruitful to bring forth the buds of righteousness. Accordingly, he is frequently called "water," as in Isaiah: "Come, all ye who thirst, to the waters" [ch. 55:1]. Also, "I shall pour out my Spirit upon him who thirsts, and rivers upon the dry land" [Isa. 44:3]. To these verses Christ's statement, quoted above, corresponds: "If anyone thirst, let him come to me" [John 7:37]. Although sometimes he is so called because of his power to cleanse and purify, as in Ezekiel, where the Lord promises "clean water" in which he will "wash away the filth" of his people [ch. 36:25].

From the fact that he restores and nourishes unto vigor of life those on whom he has poured the stream of his grace, he gets the names "oil" and "anointing" [1 John 2:20, 27]. On the other hand, persistently boiling away and burning up our vicious and inordinate desires, he enflames our hearts with the love of God and with zealous devotion. From this effect upon us he is also justly called "fire" [Luke 3:16]. In short, he is described as the "spring" [John 4:14] whence all heavenly riches flow forth to us; or as the "hand of God" [Acts 11:21], by which he exercises his might. For by the inspiration of his power he so breathes divine life into us that we are no longer actuated by ourselves, but are ruled by his action and prompting. Accordingly, whatever good things are in us are the fruits of his grace; and without him our gifts are darkness of mind and perversity of heart [cf. Gal. 5:19–21]. As has already been clearly explained, until our minds become intent upon the Spirit, Christ, so to speak, lies idle because we coldly contemplate him as outside ourselves—indeed, far from us.

III.i.4   Faith is the principal work of the Holy Spirit. Consequently, the terms commonly employed to express his power and working are, in large measure, referred to it because by faith alone he leads us into the light of the gospel.

2. FAITH

III.ii.2   Faith rests not on ignorance, but on knowledge. And this is, indeed, knowledge not only of God but of the divine will. We do not obtain salvation either because we are prepared to embrace as true whatever the church has prescribed, or because we turn over to it the task of inquiring and knowing. But we do so when we know that God is our merciful Father, because of reconciliation effected through Christ [2 Cor. 5:18–19], and that Christ has been given to us as righteousness, sanctification, and life. By this knowledge, I say, not by submission of our feeling, do we obtain entry into the Kingdom of Heaven.

III.ii.6   We must be reminded that there is a permanent relationship between faith and the Word. He could not separate one from the other any more than we could separate the rays from the sun from which they come. . . . Therefore if faith turns away even in the slightest degree from this goal toward which it should aim, it does not keep its own nature, but becomes uncertain credulity and vague error of mind. The same Word is the basis whereby faith is supported and sustained; if it turns away from the Word, it falls. Therefore, take away the Word and no faith will then remain . . . In understanding faith it is not merely a question of knowing that God exists, but also—and this especially—of knowing what is his will toward us. For it is not so much our concern to know who he is in himself, as what he wills to be toward us.

III.ii.7   Our mind must be otherwise illumined and our heart strengthened, that the Word of God may obtain full faith among us. Now we shall possess a right definition of faith if we call it a firm and certain knowledge of God's benevolence toward us, founded upon the truth of the freely given promise in Christ, both revealed to our minds and sealed upon our hearts through the Holy Spirit.

III.ii.17   While we teach that faith ought to be certain and assured, we cannot imagine any certainty that is not tinged with doubt, or any assurance that is not assailed by some anxiety. On the other hand, we say that believers are in perpetual conflict with their own unbelief. Far, indeed, are we from putting their consciences in any peaceful repose, undisturbed by any tumult at all. Yet, once again, we deny that, in whatever way they are afflicted, they fall away and depart from the certain assurance received from God's mercy. . . . He who, struggling with his own weakness, presses toward faith in his moments of anxiety is already in large part victorious.

III.ii.21   Unbelief does not hold sway within believers' hearts, but assails them from without. It does not mortally wound them with its weapons, but merely harasses them, or at most so injures them that the wound is curable.

III.ii.28   Now, in the divine benevolence, which faith is said to look to, we understand the possession of salvation and eternal life is obtained. For if, while God is favorable, no good can be lacking, when he assures us of his love we are abundantly and sufficiently assured of salvation. . . . Faith, therefore, having grasped the love of God, has promises of the present life and of that to come [1 Tim. 4:8], and firm assurance of all good things. . . . God will never fail. . . . Whatever earthly miseries and calamities await those whom God has embraced in his love, these cannot hinder his benevolence from being their full happiness.

III.ii.29   We make the freely given promise of God the foundation of faith because upon it faith properly rests. . . . Therefore, if we would not have our faith tremble and waver, we must buttress it with the promise of salvation, which is willingly and freely offered to us by the Lord in consideration of our misery rather than our deserts.

III.ii.33   Our mind has such an inclination to vanity that it can never cleave fast to the truth of God; and it has such a dullness that it is always blind to the light of God's truth. Accordingly, without the illumination of the Holy Spirit, the Word can do nothing. From this, also, it is clear that faith is much higher than human understanding. And it will not be enough for the mind to be illumined by the Spirit of God unless the heart is also strengthened and supported by his power.... In both ways, therefore, faith is a singular gift of God, both in that the mind of man is purged so as to be able to taste the truth of God and in that his heart is established therein. For the Spirit is not only the initiator of faith, but increases it by degrees, until by it he leads us to the Kingdom of Heaven.

III.ii.34   As we cannot come to Christ unless we be drawn by the Spirit of God, so when we are drawn we are lifted up in mind and heart above our understanding. For the soul, illumined by him, takes on a new keenness, as it were, to contemplate the heavenly mysteries, whose splendor had previously blinded it.... The Word of God is like the sun, shining upon all those to whom it is proclaimed, but with no effect among the blind. Now, all of us are blind by nature in this respect. Accordingly, it cannot penetrate into our minds unless the Spirit, as the inner teacher, through his illumination makes entry for it.

III.ii.36   It now remains to pour into the heart itself what the mind has absorbed. For the Word of God is not received by faith if it flits about in the top of the brain, but when it takes root in the depth of the heart that it may be an invincible defense to withstand and drive off all the strategems of temptation.... The Spirit accordingly serves as a seal, to seal up in our hearts those very promises the certainty of which it has previously impressed upon our minds; and takes the place of a guarantee to confirm and establish them.

III.ii.42   Wherever this faith is alive, it must have along with it the hope of eternal salvation as its inseparable companion. Or rather, it engenders and brings forth hope from itself. When this hope is taken away, however eloquently or elegantly we discourse concerning faith, we are convicted of having none.... Hope is nothing else than the expectation of those things which faith has believed to have been truly promised by God. Thus, faith believes God to be true, hope awaits the time when his truth shall be manifested; faith believes that he is our Father, hope anticipates that he will ever show himself to be a Father toward us; faith believes that eternal life has been given to us, hope anticipates that it will some time be revealed; faith is the foundation upon which hope rests, hope nourishes and sustains faith.

3. REPENTANCE

III.iii.1   Even though we have taught in part how faith pos-
sesses Christ, and how through it we enjoy his benefits, this would still remain obscure if we did not add an
explanation of the effects we feel. . . . Now it ought to be a fact
beyond controversy that repentance not only constantly follows faith, but is also born of faith. . . . No one can embrace the
grace of the gospel without betaking himself from the errors
of his past life into the right way, and applying his whole effort
to the practice of repentance. There are some, however, who
suppose that repentance precedes faith, rather than flows from
it, or is produced by it as fruit from a tree. Such persons have
never known the power of repentance, and are moved to feel
this way by an unduly slight argument.

III.iii.2   Christ, they say, and John in their preaching first urge
the people to repentance, then add that the Kingdom
of Heaven has come near [Matt. 3:2; 4:17]. . . . Yet while they
superstitiously cling to the joining together of syllables, they
disregard the meaning that binds these words together. . . . A
man cannot apply himself seriously to repentance without
knowing himself to belong to God. But no one is truly persuaded that he belongs to God unless he has first recognized
God's grace. These matters will be more clearly discussed in
what follows.

III.iii.3   But certain men well versed in penance, even long
before these times, meaning to speak simply and sin-
cerely according to the rule of Scripture, said that it consists
of two parts: mortification and vivification. Mortification they
explain as sorrow of soul and dread conceived from the recognition of sin and the awareness of divine judgment. . . . "Vivification" they understand as the consolation that arises out of
faith.

III.iii.5   Although all these things are true, yet the word "repentance" itself, so far as I can learn from Scripture,
is to be understood otherwise. For their inclusion of faith
under repentance disagrees with what Paul says in Acts: "Testifying both to Jews and Gentiles of repentance to God, and of
faith . . . in Jesus Christ" [Acts 20:21]. There he reckons repentance and faith as two different things. What then? Can true
repentance stand, apart from faith? Not at all. But even though
they cannot be separated, they ought to be distinguished. As

faith is not without hope, yet faith and hope are different things, so repentance and faith, although they are held together by a permanent bond, require to be joined rather than confused. . . .

The Hebrew word for "repentance" is derived from conversion or return; the Greek word, from change of mind or of intention. And the thing itself corresponds closely to the etymology of both words. The meaning is that, departing from ourselves, we turn to God, and having taken off our former mind, we put on a new. On this account, in my judgment, repentance can thus be well defined: it is the true turning of our life to God, a turning that arises from a pure and earnest fear of him; and it consists in the mortification of our flesh and of the old man, and in the vivification of the Spirit.

III.iii.8   It remains for us to explain our statement that repentance consists of two parts: namely, mortification of the flesh and vivification of the spirit.

III.iii.9   Both things happen to us by participation in Christ. For if we truly partake in his death, "our old man is crucified by his power, and the body of sin perishes" [Rom. 6:6 p], that the corruption of original nature may no longer thrive. If we share in his resurrection, through it we are raised up into newness of life to correspond with the righteousness of God. Therefore, in a word, I interpret repentance as regeneration, whose sole end is to restore in us the image of God that had been disfigured and all but obliterated through Adam's transgression.

III.iii.15   It is for a very good reason that the apostle enumerates seven causes, effects, or parts in his description of repentance. They are earnestness or carefulness, excuse, indignation, fear, longing, zeal, and avenging [2 Cor. 7:11]. . . . Therefore, he says that from "sorrow . . . according to God" [2 Cor. 7:10] carefulness arises. For he who is touched with a lively feeling of dissatisfaction with self because he has sinned against his God is at the same time aroused to diligence and attention that he may escape from the devil's snares. . . . Next is "excuse," which in this passage does not signify a defense whereby the sinner, in order to escape God's judgment, either denies that he has offended or extenuates his fault; but rather purification, which relies more on asking pardon than on confidence in one's own cause. . . . There follows indignation, when the sinner moans inwardly with himself, finds fault with himself, and is angry with himself, while recognizing his own perversity and his own ungratefulness toward God.

By the word "fear" Paul means that trembling which is produced in our minds as often as we consider both what we deserve and how dreadful is the severity of God's wrath toward sinners. . . . It seems to me that he has used the word "longing" to express that diligence in doing our duty and that readiness to obey to which recognition of our sins ought especially to summon us. To this also pertains the "zeal" that he joins directly to it, for it signifies an ardor by which we are aroused. . . . For the more severe we are toward ourselves, and the more sharply we examine our own sins, the more we ought to hope that God is favorable and merciful. . . . The soul itself, stricken by dread of divine judgment, should act the part of an avenger in carrying out its own punishment. Those who are really religious experience what sort of punishments are shame, confusion, groaning, displeasure with self, and other emotions that arise out of a lively recognition of sin.

III.iii.16   Now we can understand the nature of the fruits of repentance: the duties of piety toward God, of charity toward men, and in the whole of life, holiness and purity.

XVI

THE CHRISTIAN LIFE

1. RELIGION AND LIFE

III.vi.1   The object of regeneration, as we have said, is to manifest in the life of believers a harmony and agreement between God's righteousness and their obedience, and thus to confirm the adoption that they have received as sons [Gal. 4:5; cf. 2 Peter 1:10]. The law of God contains in itself that newness by which his image can be restored in us. But because our slowness needs many goads and helps, it will be profitable to assemble from various passages of Scripture a pattern for the conduct of life in order that those who heartily repent may not err in their zeal. . . . To show the godly man how he may be directed to a rightly ordered life, and briefly to set down some universal rule with which to determine his duties—this will be quite enough for me. . . . As philosophers have fixed limits of the right and the honorable, whence they derive individual duties and the whole company of virtues, so Scripture is not without its own order in this matter, but holds to a most beautiful dispensation, and one much more certain than all the philosophical ones.

III.vi.2   This Scriptural instruction of which we speak has two main aspects. The first is that the love of righteousness, to which we are otherwise not at all inclined by nature, may be instilled and established in our hearts; the second, that a rule be set forth for us that does not let us wander about in our zeal for righteousness. There are in Scripture very many and excellent reasons for commending righteousness. . . . From what foundation may righteousness better arise than from the Scriptural warning that we must be made holy because our God is holy? [Lev. 19:2; 1 Peter 1:15–16].

III.vi.3   To wake us more effectively, Scripture shows that
            God the Father, as he has reconciled us to himself in
his Christ [cf. 2 Cor. 5:18], has in him stamped for us the
likeness [cf. Heb. 1:3] to which he would have us conform.
Now, let these persons who think that moral philosophy is duly
and systematically set forth solely among philosophers find me
among the philosophers a more excellent dispensation. They,
while they wish particularly to exhort us to virtue, announce
merely that we should live in accordance with nature. But
Scripture draws its exhortation from the true fountain. It not
only enjoins us to refer our life to God, its author, to whom it
is bound; but after it has taught that we have degenerated
from the true origin and condition of our creation, it also adds
that Christ, through whom we return into favor with God, has
been set before us as an example, whose pattern we ought to
express in our life.

III.vi.4   This is the place to upbraid those who, having nothing
            but the name and badge of Christ, yet wish to call
themselves "Christians." Yet, how shamelessly do they boast of
his sacred name? Indeed, there is no intercourse with Christ
save for those who have perceived the right understanding of
Christ from the word of the gospel. . . . Accordingly, either let
them cease to boast of what they are not, in contempt of God;
or let them show themselves disciples not unworthy of Christ
their teacher.

III.vi.5   I do not insist that the moral life of a Christian man
            breathe nothing but the very gospel, yet this ought to
be desired, and we must strive toward it. But I do not so strictly
demand evangelical perfection that I would not acknowledge
as a Christian one who has not yet attained it. For thus all
would be excluded from the church, since no one is found who
is not far removed from it, while many have advanced a little
toward it whom it would nevertheless be unjust to cast away.
    What then? Let that target be set before our eyes at which
we are earnestly to aim. Let that goal be appointed toward
which we should strive and struggle. For it is not lawful for you
to divide things with God in such a manner that you undertake
part of those things which are enjoined upon you by his Word
but omit part, according to your own judgment. For in the first
place, he everywhere commends integrity as the chief part of
worshiping him [Gen. 17:1; Ps. 41:12; etc.]. By this word he
means a sincere simplicity of mind, free from guile and feign-
ing, the opposite of a double heart. It is as if it were said that

the beginning of right living is spiritual, where the inner feeling of the mind is unfeignedly dedicated to God for the cultivation of holiness and righteousness.

But no one in this earthly prison of the body has sufficient strength to press on with due eagerness, and weakness so weighs down the greater number that, with wavering and limping and even creeping along the ground, they move at a feeble rate. Let each one of us, then, proceed according to the measure of his puny capacity and set out upon the journey we have begun. No one shall set out so inauspiciously as not daily to make some headway, though it be slight. Therefore, let us not cease so to act that we may make some unceasing progress in the way of the Lord. And let us not despair at the slightness of our success; for even though attainment may not correspond to desire, when today outstrips yesterday the effort is not lost. Only let us look toward our mark with sincere simplicity and aspire to our goal; not fondly flattering ourselves, nor excusing our own evil deeds, but with continuous effort striving toward this end: that we may surpass ourselves in goodness until we attain to goodness itself. It is this, indeed, which through the whole course of life we seek and follow. But we shall attain it only when we have cast off the weakness of the body, and are received into full fellowship with him.

2. CHRISTIAN SELF-DENIAL

III.vii.1 Even though the law of the Lord provides the finest and best-disposed method of ordering a man's life, it seemed good to the Heavenly Teacher to shape his people by an even more explicit plan to that rule which he had set forth in the law. Here, then, is the beginning of this plan: the duty of believers is "to present their bodies to God as a living sacrifice, holy and acceptable to him," and in this consists the lawful worship of him [Rom. 12:1] . . .

We are not our own: let not our reason nor our will, therefore, sway our plans and deeds. We are not our own: let us therefore not set it as our goal to seek what is expedient for us according to the flesh. We are not our own: in so far as we can, let us therefore forget ourselves and all that is ours. Conversely, we are God's: let us therefore live for him and die for him. We are God's: let his wisdom and will therefore rule all our actions. We are God's: let all the parts of our life accordingly strive toward him as our only lawful goal [Rom. 14:8; cf. 1 Cor. 6:19]. . . . Let this therefore be the first step, that a man depart from himself in order that he may apply the whole force of his ability in the service of the Lord. I call "service" not only what lies in obedience to God's Word but what turns the mind of man, empty of its own carnal sense, wholly to the bidding of God's Spirit.

III.vii.2   From this also follows this second point: that we seek not the things that are ours but those which are of the Lord's will and will serve to advance his glory.

III.vii.4   Whatever man we deal with, we shall treat him not only moderately and modestly but also cordially and as a friend. You will never attain true gentleness except by one path: a heart imbued with lowliness and with reverence for others.

III.vii.5   No surer rule and no more valid exhortation to keep it could be devised than when we are taught that all the gifts we possess have been bestowed by God and entrusted to us on condition that they be distributed for our neighbors' benefit [cf. 1 Peter 4:10]. . . . We are the stewards of everything God has conferred on us by which we are able to help our neighbor, and are required to render account of our stewardship. Moreover, the only right stewardship is that which is tested by the rule of love.

III.vii.6   Furthermore, not to grow weary in well-doing [Gal. 6:9], which otherwise must happen immediately, we ought to add that other idea which the apostle mentions: "Love is patient . . . and is not irritable" [1 Cor. 13:4–5]. . . . Assuredly there is but one way in which to achieve what is not merely difficult but utterly against human nature: to love those who hate us, to repay their evil deeds with benefits, to return blessings for reproaches [Matt. 5:44]. It is that we remember not to consider men's evil intention but to look upon the image of God in them, which cancels and effaces their transgressions, and with its beauty and dignity allures us to love and embrace them.

III.vii.7   This mortification, then, will take place in us only if we fulfill the duties of love. Now he who merely performs all the duties of love does not fulfill them, even though he overlooks none; but he, rather, fulfills them who does this from a sincere feeling of love. For it can happen that one who indeed discharges to the full all his obligations as far as outward duties are concerned is still all the while far away from the true way of discharging them.

III.vii.9   Suppose we believe that every means toward a pros-
           perous and desirable outcome rests upon the blessing
of God alone; and that, when this is absent, all sorts of misery
and calamity dog us. It remains for us not greedily to strive
after riches and honors—whether relying upon our own dex-
terity of wit or our own diligence, or depending upon the favor
of men, or having confidence in vainly imagined fortune—but
for us always to look to the Lord so that by his guidance we may
be led to whatever lot he has provided for us. Thus it will first
come to pass that we shall not dash out to seize upon riches and
usurp honors through wickedness and by stratagems and evil
arts, or greed, to the injury of our neighbors; but pursue only
those enterprises which do not lead us away from innocence.
. . . Then will a bridle be put on us that we may not burn with
an immoderate desire to grow rich or ambitiously pant after
honors. . . . If things do not go according to our wish and hope,
we will still be restrained from impatience and loathing of our
condition, whatever it may be.

III.vii.10   For godly minds the peace and forbearance we have
            spoken of ought not to rest solely in this point; but it
must also be extended to every occurrence to which the present life is subject. Therefore, he alone has duly denied himself
who has so totally resigned himself to the Lord that he permits
every part of his life to be governed by God's will. He who will
be thus composed in mind, whatever happens, will not consider himself miserable nor complain of his lot with ill will
toward God.

III.viii.1   Whomever the Lord has adopted and deemed worthy
           of his fellowship ought to prepare themselves for a
hard, toilsome, and unquiet life, crammed with very many and
various kinds of evil. It is the Heavenly Father's will thus to
exercise them so as to put his own children to a definite test.

III.viii.2   Our Lord had no need to undertake the bearing of the
           cross except to attest and prove his obedience to the
Father. But as for us, there are many reasons why we must pass
our lives under a continual cross. . . . We readily esteem our
virtue above its due measure. And we do not doubt, whatever
happens, that against all difficulties it will remain unbroken
and unconquered. Hence we are lifted up into stupid and

empty confidence in the flesh; and relying on it, we are then insolently proud against God himself, as if our own powers were sufficient without his grace.

He can best restrain this arrogance when he proves to us by experience not only the great incapacity but also the frailty under which we labor. Therefore, he afflicts us either with disgrace or poverty, or bereavement, or disease, or other calamities. Utterly unequal to bearing these, in so far as they touch us, we soon succumb to them. Thus humbled, we learn to call upon his power, which alone makes us stand fast under the weight of afflictions.

III.viii.4   The Lord also has another purpose for afflicting his people: to test their patience and to instruct them to obedience. Not that they can manifest any other obedience to him save what he has given them. But it so pleases him by unmistakable proofs to make manifest and clear the graces which he has conferred upon the saints, that these may not lie idle, hidden within.

III.viii.7   Now, to suffer persecution for righteousness' sake is a singular comfort. For it ought to occur to us how much honor God bestows upon us in thus furnishing us with the special badge of his soldiery. . . . If, being innocent and of good conscience, we are stripped of our possessions by the wickedness of impious folk, we are indeed reduced to penury among men. But in God's presence in heaven our true riches are thus increased. If we are cast out of our own house, then we will be the more intimately received into God's family. If we are vexed and despised, we but take all the firmer root in Christ. If we are branded with disgrace and ignominy, we but have a fuller place in the Kingdom of God. If we are slain, entrance into the blessed life will thus be open to us. Let us be ashamed to esteem less than the shadowy and fleeting allurements of the present life, those things on which the Lord has set so great a value.

3. THE GOOD LIFE AND THE LIFE TO COME

III.ix.1   Whatever kind of tribulation presses upon us, we must ever look to this end: to accustom ourselves to contempt for the present life and to be aroused thereby to meditate upon the future life. . . . There is not one of us, indeed, who does not wish to seem throughout his life to aspire and strive after heavenly immortality. For it is a shame for us to be no better than brute beasts, whose condition would be no whit inferior to our own if there were not left to us hope of eternity after death. But if you examine the plans, the efforts, the deeds, of anyone, there you will find nothing else but earth.

The whole soul, enmeshed in the allurements of the flesh, seeks its happiness on earth. To counter this evil the Lord instructs his followers in the vanity of the present life by continual proof of its miseries. Therefore, that they may not promise themselves a deep and secure peace in it, he permits them often to be troubled and plagued either with wars or tumults, or robberies, or other injuries. That they may not pant with too great eagerness after fleeting and transient riches, or repose in those which they possess, he sometimes by exile, sometimes by barrenness of the earth, sometimes by fire, sometimes by other means, reduces them to poverty, or at least confines them to a moderate station. That they may not too complacently take delight in the goods of marriage, he either causes them to be troubled by the depravity of their wives or humbles them by evil offspring, or afflicts them with bereavement. But if, in all these matters, he is more indulgent toward them, yet, that they may not either be puffed up with vainglory or exult in self-assurance, he sets before their eyes, through diseases and perils, how unstable and fleeting are all the goods that are subject to mortality.

Then only do we rightly advance by the discipline of the cross, when we learn that this life, judged in itself, is troubled, turbulent, unhappy in countless ways, and in no respect clearly happy; that all those things which are judged to be its goods are uncertain, fleeting, vain, and vitiated by many intermingled evils. From this, at the same time, we conclude that in this life we are to seek and hope for nothing but struggle; when we think of our crown, we are to raise our eyes to heaven.

III.ix.3　　Let believers accustom themselves to a contempt of the present life that engenders no hatred of it or ingratitude against God. Indeed, this life, however crammed with infinite miseries it may be, is still rightly to be counted among those blessings of God which are not to be spurned. . . .

We begin in the present life, through various benefits, to taste the sweetness of the divine generosity in order to whet our hope and desire to seek after the full revelation of this. When we are certain that the earthly life we live is a gift of

God's kindness, as we are beholden to him for it we ought to remember it and be thankful. Then we shall come in good time to consider its most unhappy condition in order that we may, indeed, be freed from too much desire of it, to which, as has been said, we are of ourselves inclined by nature.

III.ix.4 Let the aim of believers in judging mortal life, then, be that while they understand it to be of itself nothing but misery, they may with greater eagerness and dispatch betake themselves wholly to meditate upon that eternal life to come. When it comes to a comparison with the life to come, the present life can not only be safely neglected but, compared to the former, must be utterly despised and loathed. For, if heaven is our homeland, what else is the earth but our place of exile? If departure from the world is entry into life, what else is the world but a sepulcher? And what else is it for us to remain in life but to be immersed in death? If to be freed from the body is to be released into perfect freedom, what else is the body but a prison? If to enjoy the presence of God is the summit of happiness, is not to be without this, misery? But until we leave the world "we are away from the Lord" [2 Cor. 5:6]. Therefore, if the earthly life be compared with the heavenly, it is doubtless to be at once despised and trampled under foot. Of course it is never to be hated except in so far as it holds us subject to sin; although not even hatred of that condition may ever properly be turned against life itself. In any case, it is still fitting for us to be so affected either by weariness or hatred of it that, desiring its end, we may also be prepared to abide in it at the Lord's pleasure, so that our weariness may be far from all murmuring and impatience. For it is like a sentry post at which the Lord has posted us, which we must hold until he recalls us.

4. RULES FOR CHRISTIAN LIVING

III.x.2 Let this be our principle: that the use of God's gifts is not wrongly directed when it is referred to that end to which the Author himself created and destined them for us, since he created them for our good, not for our ruin. . . . Has the Lord clothed the flowers with the great beauty that greets our eyes, the sweetness of smell that is wafted upon our nostrils, and yet will it be unlawful for our eyes to be affected by that beauty, or our sense of smell by the sweetness of that odor? What? Did he not so distinguish colors as to make some more lovely than others? What? Did he not endow gold and silver, ivory and marble, with a loveliness that renders them more precious than other metals or stones? Did he not, in short, render many things attractive to us, apart from their necessary use?

III.x.3 Away, then, with that inhuman philosophy which, while conceding only a necessary use of creatures, not only malignantly deprives us of the lawful fruit of God's beneficence but cannot be practiced unless it robs a man of all his senses and degrades him to a block. But no less diligently, on the other hand, we must resist the lust of the flesh, which, unless it is kept in order, overflows without measure.

III.x.4 Even though the freedom of believers in external matters is not to be restricted to a fixed formula, yet it is surely subject to this law: to indulge oneself as little as possible: but, on the contrary, with unflagging effort of mind to insist upon cutting off all show of superfluous wealth, not to mention licentiousness, and diligently to guard against turning helps into hindrances.

III.x.5 The second rule will be: they who have narrow and slender resources should know how to go without things patiently, lest they be troubled by an immoderate desire for them. . . . Besides, Scripture has a third rule with which to regulate the use of earthly things. Of it we said something when we discussed the precepts of love. It decrees that all those things were so given to us by the kindness of God, and so destined for our benefit, that they are, as it were, entrusted to us, and we must one day render account of them.

III.x.6 Finally, this point is to be noted: the Lord bids each one of us in all life's actions to look to his calling. For he knows with what great restlessness human nature flames, with what fickleness it is borne hither and thither, how its ambition longs to embrace various things at once. Therefore, lest through our stupidity and rashness everything be turned topsy-turvy, he has appointed duties for every man in his particular way of life. And that no one may thoughtlessly transgress his limits, he has named these various kinds of living "callings." Therefore each individual has his own kind of living assigned to him by the Lord as a sort of sentry post so that he may not heedlessly wander about throughout life.

XVII

JUSTIFICATION BY FAITH

1. JUSTIFICATION BY FAITH DEFINED

III.xi.1 Christ was given to us by God's generosity, to be grasped and possessed by us in faith. By partaking of him, we principally receive a double grace: namely, that being reconciled to God through Christ's blamelessness, we may have in heaven instead of a Judge a gracious Father; and secondly, that sanctified by Christ's spirit we may cultivate blamelessness and purity of life. Of regeneration, indeed, the second of these gifts, I have said what seemed sufficient. The theme of justification was therefore more lightly touched upon because it was more to the point to understand first how little devoid of good works is the faith, through which alone we obtain free righteousness by the mercy of God; and what is the nature of the good works of the saints, with which part of this question is concerned. Therefore we must now discuss these matters thoroughly. And we must so discuss them as to bear in mind that this is the main hinge on which religion turns.

III.xi.2 But that we may not stumble on the very threshold—and this would happen if we should enter upon a discussion of a thing unknown—first let us explain what these expressions mean: that man is justified in God's sight, and that he is justified by faith or works. He is said to be justified in God's sight who is both reckoned righteous in God's judgment and has been accepted on account of his righteousness. Indeed, as iniquity is abominable to God, so no sinner can find favor in his eyes in so far as he is a sinner and so long as he is reckoned as such. Accordingly, wherever there is sin, there also the wrath and vengeance of God show themselves. Now he is justified who is reckoned in the condition not of a sinner, but of a righteous man; and for that reason, he stands firm before God's judgment seat while all sinners fall. . . .

Thus, justified before God is the man who, freed from the company of sinners, has God to witness and affirm his righteousness. In the same way, therefore, he in whose life that purity and holiness will be found which deserves a testimony of righteousness before God's throne will be said to be justified by works, or else he who, by the wholeness of his works, can meet and satisfy God's judgment. On the contrary, justified by faith is he who, excluded from the righteousness of works, grasps the righteousness of Christ through faith, and clothed in it, appears in God's sight not as a sinner but as a righteous man. Therefore, we explain justification simply as the acceptance with which God receives us into his favor as righteous men. And we say that it consists in the remission of sins and the imputation of Christ's righteousness.

III.xi.3 There are many clear testimonies of Scripture to confirm this fact. First, it cannot be denied that this is a proper and most customary meaning of the word. But because it would take too long to collect all the passages and to compare them, let it suffice to have called them to our readers' attention, for they will readily observe such of themselves. I shall bring forward only a few, where this justification of which we are speaking is expressly treated.

III.xi.13 But a great part of mankind imagine that righteousness is composed of faith and works. Let us also, to begin with, show that faith righteousness so differs from works righteousness that when one is established the other has to be overthrown. . . . If by establishing our own righteousness we shake off the righteousness of God, to attain the latter we must indeed completely do away with the former. . . . So long as any particle of works righteousness remains some occasion for boasting remains with us. Now, if faith excludes all boasting, works righteousness can in no way be associated with faith righteousness. . . . Farewell, then, to the dream of those who think up a righteousness flowing together out of faith and works.

III.xi.16 This is the experience of faith through which the sinner comes into possession of his salvation when from the teaching of the gospel he acknowledges that he has been reconciled to God: that with Christ's righteousness interceding and forgiveness of sins accomplished he is justified. And although regenerated by the Spirit of God, he ponders the everlasting righteousness laid up for him not in the good works to which he inclines but in the sole righteousness of Christ.

III.xi.17   We should recall to mind the relation that we have previously established between faith and the gospel. For faith is said to justify because it receives and embraces the righteousness offered in the gospel. Moreover, because righteousness is said to be offered through the gospel, all consideration of works is excluded.

III.xi.18   Faith receives that righteousness which the gospel bestows. The gospel differs from the law in that it does not link righteousness to works but lodges it solely in God's mercy.

III.xi.21   Now let us examine how true that statement is which is spoken in the definition, that the righteousness of faith is reconciliation with God, which consists solely in the forgiveness of sins. . . . Sin is division between man and God, the turning of God's face away from the sinner; and it cannot happen otherwise, seeing that it is foreign to his righteousness to have any dealings with sin. For this reason, the apostle teaches that man is God's enemy until he is restored to grace through Christ [Rom. 5:8–10]. Thus, him whom he receives into union with himself the Lord is said to justify, because he cannot receive him into grace nor join him to himself unless he turns him from a sinner into a righteous man. We add that this is done through forgiveness of sins; for if those whom the Lord has reconciled to himself be judged by works, they will indeed still be found sinners, though they ought, nevertheless, to be freed and cleansed from sin. It is obvious, therefore, that those whom God embraces are made righteous solely by the fact that they are purified when their spots are washed away by forgiveness of sins. Consequently, such righteousness can be called, in a word, "remission of sins."

III.xi.23   From this it is also evident that we are justified before God solely by the intercession of Christ's righteousness. This is equivalent to saying that man is not righteous in himself but because the righteousness of Christ is communicated to him by imputation—something worth carefully noting. Indeed, that frivolous notion disappears, that man is justified by faith because by Christ's righteousness he shares the Spirit of God, by whom he is rendered righteous. This is too contrary to the above doctrine ever to be reconciled to it. And there is no doubt that he who is taught to seek righteousness outside himself is destitute of righteousness in himself. Moreover, the apostle most clearly asserts this when he writes: "He who knew not sin was made the atoning sacrifice of sin for us so that we might be made the righteousness of God in him" [2 Cor. 5:21 p]. You see that our righteousness is not in us but in Christ, that we possess it only because we are partakers in Christ; indeed, with him we possess all its riches.

III.xiii.1   Here, indeed, we are especially to note two things: namely, that the Lord's glory should stand undiminished and, so to speak, in good repair, and that our consciences in the presence of his judgment should have peaceful rest and serene tranquillity.

III.xiii.2   Thus the matter stands: we never truly glory in him unless we have utterly put off our own glory. . . . To sum up, man cannot without sacrilege claim for himself even a crumb of righteousness, for just so much is plucked and taken away from the glory of God's righteousness.

III.xiii.3   Now if we ask in what way the conscience can be made quiet before God, we shall find the only way to be that unmerited righteousness be conferred upon us as a gift of God.

III.xiii.4   Scripture shows that God's promises are not established unless they are grasped with the full assurance of conscience. Wherever there is doubt or uncertainty, it pronounces them void. Again, it declares that these promises do nothing but vacillate and waver if they rest upon our own works. Therefore, righteousness must either depart from us or works must not be brought into account, but faith alone must have place, whose nature it is to prick up the ears and close the eyes—that is, to be intent upon the promise alone and to turn thought away from all worth or merit of man.

III.xiii.5   Those who prate that we are justified by faith because, being reborn, we are righteous by living spiritually have never tasted the sweetness of grace, so as to consider that God will be favorable to them. . . . Believers should be convinced that their only ground of hope for the inheritance of a

Heavenly Kingdom lies in the fact that, being engrafted in the body of Christ, they are freely accounted righteous. For, as regards justification, faith is something merely passive, bringing nothing of ours to the recovering of God's favor but receiving from Christ that which we lack.

2. WE ARE NOT SAVED
BY OUR OWN RIGHTEOUSNESS

III.xiv.1   To make this matter clearer, let us examine what kind of righteousness is possible to man through the whole course of his life; let us, indeed, make a fourfold classification of it. For men are either (1) endowed with no knowledge of God and immersed in idolatry, or (2) initiated into the sacraments, yet by impurity of life denying God in their actions while they confess him with their lips, they belong to Christ only in name; or (3) they are hypocrites who conceal with empty pretenses their wickedness of heart, or (4) regenerated by God's Spirit, they make true holiness their concern. In the first instance, when they are to be judged according to their natural gifts, not one spark of good will be found in them from the top of their heads to the soles of their feet.

III.xiv.2   I do not deny that all the notable endowments that manifest themselves among unbelievers are gifts of God . . . since nothing is in any way praiseworthy that does not come from him.

III.xiv.3   Yet what Augustine writes is nonetheless true: that all who are estranged from the religion of the one God, however admirable they may be regarded on account of their reputation for virtue, not only deserve no reward but rather punishment, because by the pollution of their hearts they defile God's good works. . . . When we remember the constant end of that which is right—namely, to serve God—whatever strives to another end already deservedly loses the name "right." . . . Duties are weighed not by deeds but by ends.

III.xiv.4   Whatever a man thinks, plans, or carries out before he is reconciled to God through faith is accursed, not only of no value for righteousness, but surely deserving condemnation.

III.xiv.8 We therefore hold to be beyond doubt what ought to be a mere commonplace even to one indifferently versed in the Scriptures, that in men not yet truly sanctified works manifesting even the highest splendor are so far away from righteousness before the Lord that they are reckoned sins. Accordingly, they have spoken very truly who have taught that favor with God is not obtained by anyone through works, but on the contrary works please him only when the person has previously found favor in his sight.

III.xiv.11 We must strongly insist upon these two points: first, that there never existed any work of a godly man which, if examined by God's stern judgment, would not deserve condemnation; secondly, if such a work were found (something not possible for man), it would still lose favor—weakened and stained as it is by the sins with which its author himself is surely burdened.

III.xv.3 There is no doubt that whatever is praiseworthy in works is God's grace; there is not a drop that we ought by rights to ascribe to ourselves. If we truly and earnestly recognize this, not only will all confidence in merit vanish, but the very notion. . . . Good works, then, are pleasing to God and are not unfruitful for their doers. But they receive by way of reward the most ample benefits of God, not because they so deserve but because God's kindness has of itself set this value on them.

3. JUSTIFICATION BY FAITH
AND CHRISTIAN LIBERTY

III.xix.2 Christian freedom, in my opinion, consists of three parts. The first: that the consciences of believers, in seeking assurance of their justification before God, should rise above and advance beyond the law, forgetting all law righteousness. . . . The whole life of Christians ought to be a sort of practice of godliness, for we have been called to sanctification [1 Thess. 4:7; cf. Eph. 1:4; 1 Thess. 4:3]. Here it is the function of the law, by warning men of their duty, to arouse them to a zeal for holiness and innocence. But where consciences are worried how to render God favorable, what they will reply, and with what assurance they will stand should they be called to his judgment, there we are not to reckon what the law requires, but Christ alone, who surpasses all perfection of the law, must be set forth as righteousness.

III.xix.4   The second part, dependent upon the first, is that consciences observe the law, not as if constrained by the necessity of the law, but that freed from the law's yoke they willingly obey God's will. For since they dwell in perpetual dread so long as they remain under the sway of the law, they will never be disposed with eager readiness to obey God unless they have already been given this sort of freedom.

III.xix.5   Those bound by the yoke of the law are like servants assigned certain tasks for each day by their masters. These servants think they have accomplished nothing, and dare not appear before their masters unless they have fulfilled the exact measure of their tasks. But sons, who are more generously and candidly treated by their fathers, do not hesitate to offer them incomplete and half-done and even defective works, trusting that their obedience and readiness of mind will be accepted by their fathers, even though they have not quite achieved what their fathers intended. Such children ought we to be, firmly trusting that our services will be approved by our most merciful Father, however small, rude, and imperfect these may be.

III.xix.7   The third part of Christian freedom lies in this: regarding outward things that are of themselves "indifferent," we are not bound before God by any religious obligation preventing us from sometimes using them and other times not using them, indifferently. And the knowledge of this freedom is very necessary for us, for if it is lacking, our consciences will have no repose and there will be no end to superstitions. . . . Some, in despair, are of necessity cast into a pit of confusion; others, despising God and abandoning fear of him, must make their own way in destruction.

III.xix.11   Our freedom is not given against our feeble neighbors, for love makes us their servants in all things; rather it is given that, having peace with God in our hearts, we may also live at peace with men. We learn from the Lord's words how much we ought to regard the offense of the Pharisees: He bids us let them alone because they are blind leaders of the blind [Matt. 15:14]. His disciples had warned him that the Pharisees had been offended by his talk [Matt. 15:12]. He answered that they were to be ignored and their offense disregarded.

III.xix.12 Nothing is plainer than this rule: that we should use our freedom if it results in the edification of our neighbor, but if it does not help our neighbor, then we should forgo it.

XVIII

PRAYER,
THE PRINCIPAL EXERCISE
OF FAITH

1. THE NECESSITY FOR PRAYER

III.xx.1   From those matters so far discussed, we clearly see
how destitute and devoid of all good things man is,
and how he lacks all aids to salvation. Therefore, if he seeks
resources to succor him in his need, he must go outside himself
and get them elsewhere. . . . But after we have been instructed
by faith to recognize that whatever we need and whatever we
lack is in God, and in our Lord Jesus Christ, in whom the
Father willed all the fullness of his bounty to abide [cf. Col.
1:19; John 1:16] so that we may all draw from it as from an
overflowing spring, it remains for us to seek in him, and in
prayers to ask of him, what we have learned to be in him.

III.xx.2   It is, therefore, by the benefit of prayer that we reach
those riches which are laid up for us with the Heav-
enly Father. For there is a communion of men with God by
which, having entered the heavenly sanctuary, they appeal to
him in person concerning his promises in order to experience,
where necessity so demands, that what they believed was not
vain, although he had promised it in word alone. Therefore we
see that to us nothing is promised to be expected from the
Lord, which we are not also bidden to ask of him in prayers.
So true is it that we dig up by prayer the treasures that were
pointed out by the Lord's gospel, and which our faith has
gazed upon.

Words fail to explain how necessary prayer is, and in how
many ways the exercise of prayer is profitable. Surely, with
good reason the Heavenly Father affirms that the only strong-
hold of safety is in calling upon his name [cf. Joel 2:32]. By so
doing we invoke the presence both of his providence, through

which he watches over and guards our affairs, and of his power, through which he sustains us, weak as we are and well-nigh overcome, and of his goodness, through which he receives us, miserably burdened with sins, unto grace; and, in short, it is by prayer that we call him to reveal himself as wholly present to us.

III.xx.3   But, someone will say, does God not know, even without being reminded, both in what respect we are troubled and what is expedient for us, so that it may seem in a sense superfluous that he should be stirred up by our prayers—as if he were drowsily blinking or even sleeping until he is aroused by our voice? But they who thus reason do not observe to what end the Lord instructed his people to pray, for he ordained it not so much for his own sake as for ours. . . . The holy fathers, the more confidently they extolled God's benefits among themselves and others, were the more keenly aroused to pray.

2. THE PREREQUISITES OF PRAYER

III.xx.4   Now for framing prayer duly and properly, let this be the first rule: that we be disposed in mind and heart as befits those who enter conversation with God. . . . I say that we are to rid ourselves of all alien and outside cares, by which the mind, itself a wanderer, is borne about hither and thither, drawn away from heaven, and pressed down to earth.

III.xx.5   These two matters are well worth attention: first, whoever engages in prayer should apply to it his faculties and efforts, and not, as commonly happens, be distracted by wandering thoughts. . . . We have noted another point: not to ask any more than God allows. For even though he bids us pour out our hearts before him [Ps. 62:8; cf. Ps. 145:19], he still does not indiscriminately slacken the reins to stupid and wicked emotions.

III.xx.6   Let this be the second rule: that in our petitions we ever sense our own insufficiency, and earnestly pondering how we need all that we seek, join with this prayer an earnest—nay, burning—desire to attain it. For many perfunctorily intone prayers after a set form, as if discharging a duty to God.

III.xx.7   From this it follows that only sincere worshipers of God pray aright and are heard. Let each one, therefore, as he prepares to pray be displeased with his own evil deeds, and (something that cannot happen without repentance) let him take the person and disposition of a beggar.

III.xx.8   To this let us join a third rule: that anyone who stands before God to pray, in his humility giving glory completely to God, abandon all thought of his own glory, cast off all notion of his own worth, in fine, put away all self-assurance—lest if we claim for ourselves anything, even the least bit, we should become vainly puffed up, and perish at his presence.

III.xx.9   The beginning, and even the preparation, of proper prayer is the plea for pardon with a humble and sincere confession of guilt.

III.xx.11   The fourth rule is that, thus cast down and overcome by true humility, we should be nonetheless encouraged to pray by a sure hope that our prayer will be answered. . . . It is amazing how much our lack of trust provokes God if we request of him a boon that we do not expect. Therefore nothing is more in harmony with the nature of prayers than that this rule be laid down and established for them: that they not break forth by chance but follow faith as guide.

3. CHRIST AND PRAYER

III.xx.17   Since no man is worthy to present himself to God and come into his sight, the Heavenly Father himself, to free us at once from shame and fear, which might well have thrown our hearts into despair, has given us his Son, Jesus Christ our Lord, to be our advocate [1 John 2:1] and mediator with him [1 Tim. 2:5; cf. Heb. 8:6 and 9:15], by whose guidance we may confidently come to him, and with such an intercessor, trusting nothing we ask in his name will be denied us.

III.xx.19   Now, since he is the only way, and the one access, by which it is granted us to come to God [cf. John 14:6], to those who turn aside from this way and forsake this access, no way and no access to God remain; nothing is left in his throne but wrath, judgment, and terror.

III.xx.21 Regarding the saints who, having died in the flesh, live in Christ, if we attribute any prayer to them, let us not even dream that they have any other way to petition God than through Christ, who alone is the way [John 14:6], or that their prayers are accepted by God in any other name.

III.xx.29 Constancy in prayer, even though it has especially to do with one's own private prayers, still is also concerned somewhat with the public prayers of the church. Yet these can neither be constant nor ought they even to take place otherwise than according to the polity agreed upon by common consent among all. This I grant you. For this reason, certain hours, indifferent to God but necessary for men's convenience, are agreed upon and appointed to provide for the accommodation of all, and for everything to be done "decently and in order" in the church, according to Paul's statement [1 Cor. 14:40].

III.xx.34 Now we must learn not only a more certain way of praying but also the form itself: namely, that which the Heavenly Father has taught us through his beloved Son [Matt. 6:9 ff.; Luke 11:2 ff.].

III.xx.35 This form or rule of prayer consists of six petitions. . . . Though the whole prayer is such that throughout it God's glory is to be given chief place, still the first three petitions have been particularly assigned to God's glory, and this alone we ought to look to in them, without consideration of what is called our own advantage.

III.xx.48 We have everything we ought, or are at all able, to seek of God, set forth in this form and, as it were, rule for prayer handed down by our best Master, Christ, whom the Father has appointed our teacher and to whom alone he would have us hearken [Matt. 17:5].

III.xx.50 It is fitting each one of us should set apart certain hours for this exercise. Those hours should not pass without prayer, and during them all the devotion of the heart should be completely engaged in it. These are: when we arise in the morning, before we begin daily work, when we sit down to a meal, when by God's blessing we have eaten, when we are getting ready to retire. But this must not be any superstitious observance of hours, whereby as if paying our debt to God, we imagine ourselves paid up for the remaining hours. Rather, it must be a tutelage for our weakness, which should be thus exercised and repeatedly stimulated.

III.xx.51   If, with minds composed to this obedience, we allow ourselves to be ruled by the laws of divine providence, we shall easily learn to persevere in prayer and, with desires suspended, patiently to wait for the Lord. Then we shall be sure that, even though he does not appear, he is always present to us, and will in his own time declare how he has never had ears deaf to the prayers that in men's eyes he seems to have neglected.

XIX

THE DOCTRINE OF ELECTION

1. THE DOCTRINE STATED, DIFFICULTIES INVOLVED

III.xxi.1   If it is plain that it comes to pass by God's bidding that salvation is freely offered to some while others are barred from access to it, at once great and difficult questions spring up, explicable only when reverent minds regard as settled what they may suitably hold concerning election and predestination. A baffling question this seems to many. For they think nothing more inconsistent than that out of the common multitude of men some should be predestined to salvation, others to destruction. . . . We shall never be clearly persuaded, as we ought to be, that our salvation flows from the wellspring of God's free mercy until we come to know his eternal election, which illumines God's grace by this contrast: that he does not indiscriminately adopt all into the hope of salvation but gives to some what he denies to others. . . .

But before I enter into the matter itself, I need to mention by way of preface two kinds of men. Human curiosity renders the discussion of predestination, already somewhat difficult of itself, very confusing and even dangerous. No restraints can hold it back from wandering in forbidden bypaths and thrusting upward to the heights. If allowed, it will leave no secret to God that it will not search out and unravel.

III.xxi.2   Let this, therefore, first of all be before our eyes: to seek any other knowledge of predestination than what the Word of God discloses is not less insane than if one should purpose to walk in a pathless waste [cf. Job 12:24], or to see in darkness. And let us not be ashamed to be ignorant of something in this matter, wherein there is a certain learned ignorance.

III.xxi.3   There are others who, wishing to cure this evil, all but require that every mention of predestination be buried; indeed, they teach us to avoid any question of it, as we would a reef. . . . Therefore, to hold to a proper limit in this regard also, we shall have to turn back to the Word of the Lord, in which we have a sure rule for the understanding. For Scripture is the school of the Holy Spirit, in which, as nothing is omitted that is both necessary and useful to know, so nothing is taught but what is expedient to know. Therefore we must guard against depriving believers of anything disclosed about predestination in Scripture, lest we seem either wickedly to defraud them of the blessing of their God or to accuse and scoff at the Holy Spirit for having published what it is in any way profitable to suppress.

III.xxi.4   We should not investigate what the Lord has left hidden in secret, that we should not neglect what he has brought into the open, so that we may not be convicted of excessive curiosity on the one hand, or of excessive ingratitude on the other.

III.xxi.5   No one who wishes to be thought religious dares simply deny predestination, by which God adopts some to hope of life, and sentences others to eternal death. But our opponents, especially those who make foreknowledge its cause, envelop it in numerous petty objections. We, indeed, place both doctrines in God, but we say that subjecting one to the other is absurd.

When we attribute foreknowledge to God, we mean that all things always were, and perpetually remain, under his eyes, so that to his knowledge there is nothing future or past, but all things are present. And they are present in such a way that he not only conceives them through ideas, as we have before us those things which our minds remember, but he truly looks upon them and discerns them as things placed before him. And this foreknowledge is extended throughout the universe to every creature. We call predestination God's eternal decree, by which he compacted with himself what he willed to become of each man. For all are not created in equal condition; rather, eternal life is foreordained for some, eternal damnation for others. Therefore, as any man has been created to one or the other of these ends, we speak of him as predestined to life or to death. God has attested this not only in individual persons but has given us an example of it in the whole offspring of Abraham.

III.xxi.7   As Scripture, then, clearly shows, we say that God once established by his eternal and unchangeable plan those whom he long before determined once for all to receive into salvation, and those whom, on the other hand, he would devote to destruction. We assert that, with respect to the elect, this plan was founded upon his freely given mercy, without regard to human worth; but by his just and irreprehensible but incomprehensible judgment he has barred the door of life to those whom he has given over to damnation. Now among the elect we regard the call as a testimony of election. Then we hold justification another sign of its manifestation, until they come into the glory in which the fulfillment of that election lies. But as the Lord seals his elect by call and justification, so, by shutting off the reprobate from knowledge of his name or from the sanctification of his Spirit, he, as it were, reveals by these marks what sort of judgment awaits them.

2. SCRIPTURAL BASIS OF ELECTION

III.xxii.1   Many persons dispute all these positions which we have set forth, especially the free election of believers; nevertheless, this cannot be shaken. For generally these persons consider that God distinguishes among men according as he foresees what the merits of each will be. Therefore, he adopts as sons those whom he foreknows will not be unworthy of his grace; he appoints to the damnation of death those whose dispositions he discerns will be inclined to evil intention and ungodliness. . . . Because God chooses some, and passes over others according to his own decision, they bring an action against him. . . .

Now it behooves us to pay attention to what Scripture proclaims of every person. When Paul teaches that we were chosen in Christ "before the creation of the world" [Eph. 1:4a], he takes away all consideration of real worth on our part, for it is just as if he said: since among all the offspring of Adam, the Heavenly Father found nothing worthy of his election, he turned his eyes upon his Anointed, to choose from that body as members those whom he was to take into the fellowship of life. Let this reasoning, then, prevail among believers: we were adopted in Christ into the eternal inheritance because in ourselves we were not capable of such great excellence.

III.xxii.3   If [God] chose us that we should be holy, he did not choose us because he foresaw that we would be so. For these two notions disagree: that the godly have their holiness from election, and that they arrive at election by reason of works. The quibble to which they frequently have recourse, that the Lord does not reward preceding merits with the grace of election yet grants it to future merits, has no validity. For when it is said that believers were chosen that they might be holy, at the same time it is suggested that the holiness that was to be in them originated from election.

III.xxii.7   Now let the sovereign Judge and Master give utterance on the whole question. Detecting such great hardness in his listeners that he would be almost wasting words before the crowd, in order to overcome this hindrance he cries out: "All that the Father gives me will come to me" [John 6:37]. "For this is the will of the Father, . . . that whatever he has given me, I should lose nothing of it" [John 6:39]. Note that the Father's gift is the beginning of our reception into the surety and protection of Christ. . . . Christ's words are too clear to be covered up with any clouds of evasion. "No one," he says, "can come to me unless the Father . . . draws him. . . . Everyone who has heard and learned from the Father comes to me" [John 6:44–45]. . . . This we must believe: when he declares that he knows whom he has chosen, he denotes in the human genus a particular species, distinguished not by the quality of its virtues but by heavenly decree.

From this we may infer that none excel by their own effort or diligence, seeing that Christ makes himself the Author of election. . . . To sum up: by free adoption God makes those whom he wills to be his sons; the intrinsic cause of this is in himself, for he is content with his own secret good pleasure.

III.xxii.10   Some object that God would be contrary to himself if he should universally invite all men to him but admit only a few as elect. . . . Now I deny what they claim, since it is false in two ways. For he who threatens that while it will rain upon one city there will be drought in another [Amos 4:7], and who elsewhere announces a famine of teaching [Amos 8:11], does not bind himself by a set law to call all men equally. And he who, forbidding Paul to speak the word in Asia [Acts 16:6], and turning him aside from Bithynia, draws him into Macedonia [Acts 16:7 ff.] thus shows that he has the right to distribute this treasure to whom he pleases. Through Isaiah he still more openly shows how he directs the promises of salvation specifically to the elect: for he proclaims that they alone, not the whole human race without distinction, are to become his disciples [Isa. 8:16]. Hence it is clear that the doctrine of salvation, which is said to be reserved solely and individually for the sons of the church, is falsely debased when presented as effectually profitable to all. . . . Let this suffice for the present: although the voice of the gospel addresses all in general, yet the gift of faith is rare. . . .

For seed to fall among thorns [Matt. 13:7] or on rocky ground [Matt. 13:5] is nothing new, not only because the greater part indeed show themselves obstinately disobedient to God, but because not all have been supplied with eyes and ears. How, then, shall it be consistent that God calls to himself persons who he knows will not come? . . . Faith is fitly joined to election, provided it takes second place. This order is elsewhere clearly expressed in Christ's words: "This is the will of my Father, that I should not lose what he has given. This is his will, that everyone who believes in the Son may not perish" [John 6:39–40, freely rendered].

3. EFFECTUAL CALLING

III.xxiv.1 Yet it is not without choice that God by his call manifests the election, which he otherwise holds hidden within himself; accordingly, it may properly be termed his "attestation." "For those whom he foreknew, he also appointed beforehand to be conformed to the image of his son" [Rom. 8:29]. "Those whom he appointed beforehand, he also called; those whom he called, he also justified" [Rom. 8:30] that he might sometime glorify them. Although in choosing his own the Lord already has adopted them as his children, we see that they do not come into possession of so great a good except when they are called; conversely, that when they are called, they already enjoy some share of their election. . . . But when the call is coupled with election, in this way Scripture sufficiently suggests that in it nothing but God's free mercy is to be sought. For if we ask whom he calls, and the reason why, he answers: whom he had chosen.

III.xxiv.3   But here we must beware of two errors: for some
            make man God's co-worker, to ratify election by his
consent. Thus, according to them, man's will is superior to
God's plan. As if Scripture taught that we are merely given the
ability to believe, and not, rather, faith itself! Others, although
they do not so weaken the grace of the Holy Spirit yet led by
some reason or other, make election depend upon faith, as if
it were doubtful and also ineffectual until confirmed by faith.
Indeed, that it is confirmed, with respect to us, is utterly plain;
we have also already seen that the secret plan of God, which
lay hidden, is brought to light, provided you understand by this
language merely that what was unknown is now verified—
sealed, as it were, with a seal. But it is false to say that election
takes effect only after we have embraced the gospel, and takes
its validity from this. We should indeed seek assurance of it
from this; for if we try to penetrate to God's eternal ordination,
that deep abyss will swallow us up. But when God has made
plain his ordination to us, we must climb higher, lest the effect
overwhelm the cause. For when Scripture teaches that we are
illumined according as God has chosen us, what is more absurd
and unworthy than for our eyes to be so dazzled by the brilliance of this light as to refuse to be mindful of election?

III.xxiv.5   If we seek God's fatherly mercy and kindly heart, we
            should turn our eyes to Christ, on whom alone God's
Spirit rests [cf. Matt. 3:17]. If we seek salvation, life, and the
immortality of the Heavenly Kingdom, then there is no other
to whom we may flee, seeing that he alone is the fountain of
life, the anchor of salvation, and the heir of the Kingdom of
Heaven. Now what is the purpose of election but that we,
adopted as sons by our Heavenly Father, may obtain salvation
and immortality by his favor? . . . Christ, then, is the mirror
wherein we must, and without self-deception may, contemplate our own election.

III.xxiv.6   If we desire to know whether God cares for our salva-
            tion, let us inquire whether he has entrusted us to
Christ, whom he has established as the sole Savior of all his
people. If we still doubt whether we have been received by
Christ into his care and protection, he meets that doubt when
he willingly offers himself as shepherd, and declares that we
shall be numbered among his flock if we hear his voice [John
10:3]. Let us therefore embrace Christ, who is graciously offered to us, and comes to meet us. He will reckon us in his flock
and enclose us within his fold.

III.xxiv.8   The statement of Christ "Many are called but few are
        chosen" [Matt. 22:14] is, in this manner, very badly
understood. Nothing will be ambiguous if we hold fast to what
ought to be clear from the foregoing: that there are two kinds
of call. There is the general call, by which God invites all
equally to himself through the outward preaching of the
word—even those to whom he holds it out as a savor of death
[cf. 2 Cor. 2:16], and as the occasion for severer condemnation.
The other kind of call is special, which he deigns for the most
part to give to the believers alone, while by the inward illumination of his Spirit he causes the preached Word to dwell in
their hearts. Yet sometimes he also causes those whom he
illumines only for a time to partake of it; then he justly forsakes
them on account of their ungratefulness and strikes them with
even greater blindness.

III.xxiv.10   The elect are gathered into Christ's flock by a call not
        immediately at birth, and not all at the same time, but
according as it pleases God to dispense his grace to them. But
before they are gathered unto that supreme Shepherd, they
wander scattered in the wilderness common to all; and they do
not differ at all from others except that they are protected by
God's especial mercy from rushing headlong into the final ruin
of death. If you look upon them, you will see Adam's offspring,
who savor of the common corruption of the mass. The fact that
they are not carried to utter and even desperate impiety is not
due to any innate goodness of theirs but because the eye of
God watches over their safety and his hand is outstretched to
them!

III.xxiv.11   But let what Scripture holds remain with us: "All like
        lost sheep have gone astray; every one has turned to
his own way" [Isa. 53:6], that is, to perdition. Those whom the
Lord has once determined to snatch from this gulf of destruction he defers until his own time; he only preserves them from
falling into unpardonable blasphemy.

XX

ESCHATOLOGY

1. IMMORTALITY AND THE RESURRECTION

III.xxv.1　Whatever has so far been explained concerning our salvation calls for minds lifted up to heaven, so that "we may love Christ, whom we have not seen, and believing in him may rejoice with unutterable and exalted joy" until, as Peter declares, we receive "the outcome of our faith" [1 Peter 1:8–9]. For this reason, Paul says that the faith and love of the godly have regard to the hope that rests in heaven [Col. 1:4–5]. When, therefore, with our eyes fast fixed on Christ we wait upon heaven, and nothing on earth hinders them from bearing us to the promised blessedness, the statement is truly fulfilled "that where our treasure is, our heart is" [Matt. 6:21]. Hence arises the fact that faith is so rare in this world: nothing is harder for our slowness than to climb over innumerable obstacles in "pressing on toward the goal of the upward call" [Phil. 3:14]. To the huge mass of miseries that almost overwhelms us are added the jests of profane men, which assail our innocence when we, willingly renouncing the allurements of present benefits, seem to strive after a blessedness hidden from us as if it were a fleeting shadow. Finally, above and below us, before us and behind, violent temptations besiege us, which our minds would be quite unable to sustain, were they not freed of earthly things and bound to the heavenly life, which appears to be far away. Accordingly, he alone has fully profited in the gospel who has accustomed himself to continual meditation upon the blessed resurrection.

III.xxv.3　The very importance of the matter should sharpen our attention. For Paul rightly argues that "if the dead

do not rise up again, ... the whole gospel is vain and fallacious"
[1 Cor. 15:13–14 p], for our condition would be more pitiable
than that of all other mortals [1 Cor. 15:19], seeing that, ex-
posed to the hatred and reproach of many, we are every hour
in danger [cf. 1 Cor. 15:30], yea, "we are as sheep destined for
the slaughter" [Rom. 8:36; Ps. 44:22; cf. v. 23, Comm.]. Accordingly, the authority of the gospel would fall not merely in one
part but in its entirety, which is embraced in our adoption and
the effecting of our salvation. Let us, then, be so attentive to
this most serious matter of all that no length of time may weary
us. I have deferred to this place my brief discussion of it for this
purpose: that my readers may learn, when they have received
Christ, the Author of perfect salvation, to rise up higher, and
may know that he is clothed in heavenly immortality and glory
so that the whole body may be conformed to the Head. Even
thus in his person the Holy Spirit repeatedly sets before us the
example of the resurrection.

It is difficult to believe that bodies, when consumed with
rottenness, will at length be raised up in their season. Therefore, although many of the philosophers declared souls immortal, few approved the resurrection of the flesh. Even though
there was no excuse for this point of view, we are nevertheless
reminded by it that it is something too hard for men's minds to
apprehend. Scripture provides two helps by which faith may
overcome this great obstacle: one in the parallel of Christ's
resurrection; the other in the omnipotence of God. Now whenever we consider the resurrection, let Christ's image come
before us. In the nature which he took from us he so completed
the course of mortal life that now, having obtained immortality, he is the pledge of our coming resurrection. ...

Christ rose again that he might have us as companions in the
life to come. He was raised by the Father, inasmuch as he was
Head of the church, from which the Father in no way allows
him to be severed. He was raised by the power of the Holy
Spirit, the Quickener of us in common with him. Finally, he
was raised that he might be "the resurrection and the life"
[John 11:25]. As we have said that in this mirror the living
image of the resurrection is visible to us, so is it a firm foundation to support our minds, provided we are not wearied or
irked with a longer delay; for our task is not to measure min-
utes of time as we please but patiently to wait until God in his
own good time restores his Kingdom. Paul's exhortation bears
upon this: "Christ the first fruits, then ... those who are
Christ's, each in his order" [1 Cor. 15:23].

III.xxv.4   We have said that in proving the resurrection our
              thoughts ought to be directed to God's boundless
might. Paul briefly teaches this: "To change our lowly body,"
he says, "to be like his glorious body, according to his power
which enables him . . . to subject all things to himself" [Phil.
3:21 p]. . . . But let us remember that no one is truly persuaded
of the coming resurrection unless he is seized with wonder,
and ascribes to the power of God its due glory.

2. SOME COMMON OBJECTIONS ANSWERED

III.xxv.5   Even though it was fitting for the minds of men to be
              constantly occupied in this pursuit, as if with deliber-
ate intent to blot out all memory of resurrection, death has
been called the bound of all things and the extinction of man.
Surely, Solomon expresses the commonly received opinion
when he says, "A living dog is better than a dead lion" [Eccl.
9:4]. And another passage: "Who knows whether the spirit of
man goes upward and the spirit of the beast goes downward?"
[Eccl. 3:21 p]. For in every age this brute stupidity has been
abroad, and has even forced its way into the church itself, for
the Sadducees dared publicly assert that there is no resurrection [Mark 12:18; Luke 20:27; Acts 23:8], in fact, that souls are
mortal. But in order that this gross ignorance might not excuse
anyone, by an unbelievable prompting of nature men always
had before their eyes an image of the resurrection. Why the
sacred and inviolable custom of burial but as an earnest of new
life? . . .

But Satan has not only befuddled men's senses to make them
bury with the corpses the memory of resurrection; he has also
attempted to corrupt this part of the doctrine with various
falsifications that he might at length destroy it. I pass over the
fact that in Paul's day he began to overthrow it [1 Cor. 15:12 ff.].
But a little later there followed the chiliasts, who limited the
reign of Christ to a thousand years. Now their fiction is too
childish either to need or to be worth a refutation. And the
Apocalypse, from which they undoubtedly drew a pretext for
their error, does not support them. For the number "one thousand" [Rev. 20:4] does not apply to the eternal blessedness of
the church but only to the various disturbances that awaited the
church, while still toiling on earth. On the contrary, all Scripture proclaims that there will be no end to the blessedness of
the elect or the punishment of the wicked [Matt. 25:41, 46].

Now all those matters which elude our gaze and far exceed

the capacity of our minds must either be believed as from actual oracles of God or utterly cast away. Those who assign the children of God a thousand years in which to enjoy the inheritance of the life to come do not realize how much reproach they are casting upon Christ and his Kingdom. For if they do not put on immortality, then Christ himself, to whose glory they shall be transformed, has not been received into undying glory [1 Cor. 15:13 ff.]. If their blessedness is to have an end, then Christ's Kingdom, on whose firmness it depends, is but temporary. In short, either such persons are utterly ignorant of everything divine or they are trying by a devious malice to bring to nought all the grace of God and power of Christ, the fulfillment of which is realized only when sin is blotted out, death swallowed up, and everlasting life fully restored!

III.xxv.6   Besides these, perversely curious men have brought in two other delusions. Some have thought, as if the whole man were to die, that souls would be resurrected with bodies. Others, while conceding that spirits are immortal, have held that they are to be clothed with new bodies. Thus they deny the resurrection of the flesh.

Since I have touched somewhat on the former of these notions in treating the creation of man, it will be enough to admonish my readers again what a brutish error this is: to make of the spirit, formed after the image of God, a fleeting breath, which quickens the body only in this transient life, and to annihilate the temple of the Holy Spirit; lastly, so to despoil of this gift that part of us in which the divine especially shines, and in which there are such clear tokens of immortality that the condition of the body is better and more excellent than that of the soul.

Far otherwise Scripture—which compares the body to a hut from which, it says, we depart when we die, for in this respect it considers that we differ from brute beasts. Thus Peter, near death, says the time has come to "put off" his "tent" [2 Peter 1:14]. But Paul, speaking of believers, after having said: "When our earthly house is destroyed, we have a building . . . in the heavens" [2 Cor. 5:1], adds that "we are away from the Lord as long as we remain in the body" [v. 6 p], but we long for the presence of God in the absence of the body [v. 8]. If souls did not outlive bodies, what is it that has God present when it is separated from the body? . . .

If souls when divested of their bodies did not still retain their essence, and have capacity of blessed glory, Christ would not have said to the thief: "Today you will be with me in paradise"

[Luke 23:43]. Relying on such clear testimonies, in dying let us not hesitate, after Christ's example, to entrust our souls to God [Luke 23:46], or, after Stephen's example, to commit them into Christ's keeping [Acts 7:58], who is called with good reason their faithful "Shepherd and Bishop" [1 Peter 2:25].

Now it is neither lawful nor expedient to inquire too curiously concerning our souls' intermediate state. Many torment themselves overmuch with disputing as to what place the souls occupy and whether or not they already enjoy heavenly glory. Yet it is foolish and rash to inquire concerning unknown matters more deeply than God permits us to know. Scripture goes no farther than to say that Christ is present with them, and receives them into paradise [cf. John 12:32] that they may obtain consolation, while the souls of the reprobate suffer such torments as they deserve. What teacher or master will reveal to us that which God has concealed? Concerning the place, it is no less foolish and futile to inquire, since we know that the soul does not have the same dimension as the body. . . .

Let us be content with the limits divinely set for us: namely, that the souls of the pious, having ended the toil of their warfare, enter into blessed rest, where in glad expectation they await the enjoyment of promised glory, and so all things are held in suspense until Christ the Redeemer appear.

III.xxv.7 Equally monstrous is the error of those who imagine that the souls will not receive the same bodies with which they are now clothed but will be furnished with new and different ones. . . . Nor does Scripture define anything more clearly than the resurrection of the flesh that we now bear. "For this perishable nature," says Paul, "must put on the imperishable, and this mortal nature must put on immortality" [1 Cor. 15:53]. If God made new bodies, where would this change of quality appear? . . .

Besides, if we are to be provided with new bodies, how will head and members match? Christ arose: was it by fashioning a new body for himself? No, as he had foretold, "Destroy this temple, and in three days I will raise it up" [John 2:19]. He received again the mortal body which he had previously borne. And it would not profit us much if the body which had been offered as an atoning sacrifice had been destroyed and replaced by a new one. We must hold fast to that fellowship which the apostle proclaims: that we arise because Christ arose [1 Cor. 15:12 ff.]. For nothing is less likely than that our flesh, in which we bear about the death of Christ himself, should be deprived of Christ's resurrection.

3. A PROPER ATTITUDE NECESSARY

III.xxv.8   It now remains for me to give some suggestion of the manner of resurrection. I use this language because Paul, calling it "a mystery" [1 Cor. 15:51], urges us to sobriety, and restrains us from philosophizing too freely and subtly. First, we must hold, as I have indicated, that as to substance we shall be raised again in the same flesh we now bear, but that the quality will be different. So it was that, when the same flesh of Christ which had been offered as a sacrifice was raised up, it yet excelled in other gifts as if it had become utterly different. . . .

It will not be necessary to introduce an interval of time between death and the beginning of the second life, for "in a moment, in the twinkling of an eye," the trumpet's sound will penetrate to the dead, who will be raised imperishable; and to the living, who will be suddenly changed into the same glory [1 Cor. 15:52–53].

III.xxv.10   In this matter, we must all the more, then, keep sobriety, lest forgetful of our limitations we should soar aloft with the greater boldness, and be overcome by the brightness of the heavenly glory. We also feel how we are titillated by an immoderate desire to know more than is lawful. From this, trifling and harmful questions repeatedly flow forth—trifling, I say, for from them no profit can be derived. But this second kind is worse because those who indulge in them entangle themselves in dangerous speculations; accordingly, I call these questions "harmful."

III.xxv.11   Men hungry for empty learning inquire how great the difference will be between prophets and apostles, and again, between apostles and martyrs; by how many degrees virgins will differ from married women. In short, they leave no corner of heaven exempt from their search. . . . Let this, then, be our short way out: to be satisfied with the "mirror" and its "dimness" until we see him face to face [1 Cor. 13:12]. For few out of a huge multitude care how they are to go to heaven, but all long to know beforehand what takes place there. Almost all are lazy and loath to do battle, while already picturing to themselves imaginary victories.

4. THE DESTINY OF THE UNBELIEVER

III.xxv.12 Now, because no description can deal adequately with the gravity of God's vengeance against the wicked, their torments and tortures are figuratively expressed to us by physical things, that is, by darkness, weeping, and gnashing of teeth [Matt. 8:12; 22:13], unquenchable fire [Matt. 3:12; Mark 9:43; Isa. 66:24], an undying worm gnawing at the heart [Isa. 66:24]. By such expressions the Holy Spirit certainly intended to confound all our senses with dread: as when he speaks of "a deep Gehenna prepared from eternity, fed with fire and much wood; the breath of the Lord, like a stream of brimstone, kindles it" [Isa. 30:33]. As by such details we should be enabled in some degree to conceive the lot of the wicked, so we ought especially to fix our thoughts upon this: how wretched it is to be cut off from all fellowship with God. And not that only but so to feel his sovereign power against you that you cannot escape being pressed by it. . . . What and how great is this, to be eternally and unceasingly besieged by him? On this point the Ninetieth Psalm has a memorable statement: although by his mere glance he scatters and brings to nought all mortal men, he urges his own worshipers on, the more because they are timid in this world, that he may inspire them, burdened with the cross, to press forward [Ps. 90:7 ff.], until he himself is "all in all" [1 Cor. 15:28].

BOOK FOUR

THE HOLY CATHOLIC CHURCH

XXI

THE NATURE AND FUNCTION
OF THE CHURCH

1. NATURE: THE COMMUNION OF SAINTS

IV.i.1   As explained in the previous book, it is by the faith in
the gospel that Christ becomes ours and we are made
partakers of the salvation and eternal blessedness brought by
him. Since, however, in our ignorance and sloth (to which I add
fickleness of disposition) we need outward helps to beget and
increase faith within us, and advance it to its goal, God has also
added these aids that he may provide for our weakness. And
in order that the preaching of the gospel might flourish, he
deposited this treasure in the church. He instituted "pastors
and teachers" [Eph. 4:11] through whose lips he might teach
his own; he furnished them with authority; finally, he omitted
nothing that might make for holy agreement of faith and for
right order. First of all, he instituted sacraments, which we
who have experienced them feel to be highly useful aids to
foster and strengthen faith. Shut up as we are in the prison
house of our flesh, we have not yet attained angelic rank. God,
therefore, in his wonderful providence accommodating himself to our capacity, has prescribed a way for us, though still far
off, to draw near to him. Accordingly, our plan of instruction
now requires us to discuss the church, its government, orders,
and power; then the sacraments; and lastly, the civil order.

IV.i.2   The article in the Creed in which we profess to "believe the church" refers not only to the visible church
(our present topic) but also to all God's elect, in whose number
are also included the dead. The word "believe" is used because
often no other distinction can be made between God's children and the ungodly, between his own flock and wild beasts.
There is no good reason why many insert the preposition "in."

I admit that it is more usual and is not without the support of antiquity. . . . We testify that we believe *in* God because our mind reposes in him as truthful, and our trust rests in him. To say "*in* the church" would be as inappropriate as "*in* the forgiveness of sins" or "*in* the resurrection of the body." Consequently, although I do not wish to dispute over words, I should prefer to use the proper phrase, one better fitted to express the matter, rather than to affect forms of speaking which needlessly obscure it. . . .

The church is called "catholic," or "universal," because there could not be two or three churches unless Christ be torn asunder [cf. 1 Cor. 1:13]—which cannot happen! But all the elect are so united in Christ [cf. Eph. 1:22–23] that as they are dependent on one Head, they also grow together into one body, being joined and knit together [cf. Eph. 4:16] as are the limbs of a body [Rom. 12:5; 1 Cor. 10:17; 12:12, 27]. They are made truly one since they live together in one faith, hope, and love, and in the same Spirit of God. For they have been called not only into the same inheritance of eternal life but also to participate in one God and Christ [Eph. 5:30].

IV.i.3   This article of the Creed also applies to some extent
              to the outward church, in that each of us should keep
in brotherly agreement with all God's children, should yield to the church the authority it deserves, in short, should act as one of the flock. Accordingly, "the communion of saints" is added. This clause, though generally omitted by the ancients, ought not to be overlooked, for it very well expresses what the church is. It is as if one said that the saints are gathered into the society of Christ on the principle that whatever benefits God confers upon them, they should in turn share with one another. . . .

Now, it is very important for us to know what benefit we shall gain from this. The basis on which we believe the church is that we are fully convinced we are members of it. In this way our salvation rests upon sure and firm supports, so that, even if the whole fabric of the world were overthrown, the church could neither totter nor fall. First, it stands by God's election, and cannot waver or fail any more than his eternal providence can. Secondly, it has in a way been joined to the steadfastness of Christ, who will no more allow his believers to be estranged from him than that his members be rent and torn asunder. Besides, we are certain that, while we remain within the bosom of the church, the truth will always abide with us. Finally, we feel that these promises apply to us: "There will be salvation in Zion" [Joel 2:32; Obad. 17; cf. Vg.]; "God will abide in the midst of Jerusalem forever, that it may never be moved" [Ps. 46:5]. So powerful is participation in the church that it keeps us in the society of God. In the very word "communion" there is a wealth of comfort because, while it is determined that whatever the Lord bestows upon his members and ours belongs to us, our hope is strengthened by all the benefits they receive.

Yet, to embrace the unity of the church in this way, we need not (as we have said) see the church with the eyes or touch it with the hands. Rather, the fact that it belongs to the realm of faith should warn us to regard it no less since it passes our understanding than if it were clearly visible. And our faith is no worse because it recognizes a church beyond our ken. For here we are not bidden to distinguish between reprobate and elect—that is for God alone, not for us, to do—but to establish with certainty in our hearts that all those who, by the kindness of God the Father, through the working of the Holy Spirit, have entered into fellowship with Christ, are set apart as God's property and personal possession; and that when we are of their number we share that great grace.

IV.i.4　　But because it is now our intention to discuss the visible church, let us learn even from the simple title "mother" how useful, indeed how necessary, it is that we should know her. For there is no other way to enter into life unless this mother conceive us in her womb, give us birth, nourish us at her breast, and lastly, unless she keep us under her care and guidance until, putting off mortal flesh, we become like the angels [Matt. 22:30]. Our weakness does not allow us to be dismissed from her school until we have been pupils all our lives. Furthermore, away from her bosom one cannot hope for any forgiveness of sins or any salvation, as Isaiah [Isa. 37:32] and Joel [Joel 2:32] testify.

IV.i.5　　But let us proceed to set forth what pertains to this topic. Paul writes that Christ, "that he might fill all things," appointed some to be "apostles, some prophets, some evangelists, some pastors and teachers, for the equipment of the saints, for the work of the ministry, for the building up of the body of Christ, until we all reach the unity of the faith and of the knowledge of the Son of God, to perfect manhood, to the measure of the fully mature age of Christ" [Eph. 4:10–13, Comm., but cf. also Vg.]. We see how God, who could in a moment perfect his own, nevertheless desires them to grow up into manhood solely under the education of the church. We see the way set for it: the preaching of the heavenly doctrine has been enjoined upon the pastors. We see that all are brought under the same regulation, that with a gentle and teachable spirit they may allow themselves to be governed by teachers appointed to this function. . . .

As [God] was of old not content with the law alone, but added priests as interpreters from whose lips the people might ask its true meaning [cf. Mal. 2:7], so today he not only desires us to be attentive to its reading, but also appoints instructors to help us by their effort. This is doubly useful. On the one hand, he proves our obedience by a very good test when we hear his ministers speaking just as if he himself spoke. On the other, he also provides for our weakness in that he prefers to address us in human fashion through interpreters in order to draw us to himself, rather than to thunder at us and drive us away. Indeed, from the dread with which God's majesty justly overwhelms them, all the pious truly feel how much this familiar sort of teaching is needed.

Those who think the authority of the Word is dragged down by the baseness of the men called to teach it disclose their own ungratefulness. For, among the many excellent gifts with which God has adorned the human race, it is a singular privilege that he deigns to consecrate to himself the mouths and tongues of men in order that his voice may resound in them. . . .

Many are led either by pride, dislike, or rivalry to the conviction that they can profit enough from private reading and meditation; hence they despise public assemblies and deem preaching superfluous. But, since they do their utmost to sever or break the sacred bond of unity, no one escapes the just penalty of this unholy separation without bewitching himself with pestilent errors and foulest delusions.

IV.i.7   Holy Scripture speaks of the church in two ways. Sometimes by the term "church" it means that which is actually in God's presence, into which no persons are received but those who are children of God by grace of adoption and true members of Christ by sanctification of the Holy Spirit. Then, indeed, the church includes not only the saints presently living on earth, but all the elect from the beginning of the world. Often, however, the name "church" designates the whole multitude of men spread over the earth who profess to worship one God and Christ. By baptism we are initiated into faith in him; by partaking in the Lord's Supper we attest our unity in true doctrine and love; in the Word of the Lord we have agreement, and for the preaching of the Word the ministry instituted by Christ is preserved. In this church are mingled many hypocrites who have nothing of Christ but the name and outward appearance. There are very many ambitious, greedy, envious persons, evil speakers, and some of quite unclean life. Such are tolerated for a time either because they cannot be convicted by a competent tribunal or because a vigorous discipline does not always flourish as it ought.

Just as we must believe, therefore, that the former church, invisible to us, is visible to the eyes of God alone, so we are commanded to revere and keep communion with the latter, which is called "church" in respect to men.

IV.i.8 We recognize as members of the church those who, by confession of faith, by example of life, and by partaking of the sacraments, profess the same God and Christ with us. He has, moreover, set off by plainer marks the knowledge of his very body to us, knowing how necessary it is to our salvation.

IV.i.9 From this the face of the church comes forth and becomes visible to our eyes. Wherever we see the Word of God purely preached and heard, and the sacraments administered according to Christ's institution, there, it is not to be doubted, a church of God exists [cf. Eph. 2:20]. For his promise cannot fail: "Wherever two or three are gathered in my name, there I am in the midst of them" [Matt. 18:20].

But that we may clearly grasp the sum of this matter, we must proceed by the following steps: the church universal is a multitude gathered from all nations; it is divided and dispersed in separate places, but agrees on the one truth of divine doctrine, and is bound by the bond of the same religion. Under it are thus included individual churches, disposed in towns and villages according to human need, so that each rightly has the name and authority of the church. Individual men who, by their profession of religion, are reckoned within such churches, even though they may actually be strangers to the church, still in a sense belong to it until they have been rejected by public judgment.

There is, however, a slightly different basis for judgment concerning individual men and churches. For it may happen that we ought to treat like brothers and count as believers those whom we think unworthy of the fellowship of the godly, because of the common agreement of the church by which they are borne and tolerated in the body of Christ. We do not by our vote approve such persons as members of the church, but we leave to them such place as they occupy among the people of God until it is lawfully taken from them.

But we must think otherwise of the whole multitude itself. If it has the ministry of the Word and honors it, if it has the administration of the sacraments, it deserves without doubt to be held and considered a church. For it is certain that such things are not without fruit. In this way we preserve for the universal church its unity, which devilish spirits have always tried to sunder; and we do not defraud of their authority those lawful assemblies which have been set up in accordance with local needs.

IV.i.12   The pure ministry of the Word and pure mode of celebrating the sacraments are, as we say, sufficient pledge and guarantee that we may safely embrace as church any society in which both these marks exist. The principle extends to the point that we must not reject it so long as it retains them, even if it otherwise swarms with many faults. What is more, some fault may creep into the administration of either doctrine or sacraments, but this ought not to estrange us from communion with the church. For not all the articles of true doctrine are of the same sort. Some are so necessary to know that they should be certain and unquestioned by all men as the proper principles of religion. Such are: God is one; Christ is God and the Son of God; our salvation rests in God's mercy; and the like. Among the churches there are other articles of doctrine disputed which still do not break the unity of faith. . . .

Does this not sufficiently indicate that a difference of opinion over these nonessential matters should in no wise be the basis of schism among Christians? First and foremost, we should agree on all points. But since all men are somewhat beclouded with ignorance, either we must leave no church remaining, or we must condone delusion in those matters which can go unknown without harm to the sum of religion and without loss of salvation.

But here I would not support even the slightest errors with the thought of fostering them through flattery and connivance. But I say we must not thoughtlessly forsake the church because of any petty dissensions. For in it alone is kept safe and uncorrupted that doctrine in which piety stands sound and the use of the sacraments ordained by the Lord is guarded. In the meantime, if we try to correct what displeases us, we do so out of duty. Paul's statement applies to this: "If a better revelation is made to another sitting by, let the first be silent" [1 Cor. 14:30 p]. From this it is clear that every member of the church is charged with the responsibility of public edification according to the measure of his grace, provided he perform it decently and in order. That is, we are neither to renounce the communion of the church nor, remaining in it, to disturb its peace and duly ordered discipline.

IV.i.16   For because God willed that the communion of his church be maintained in this outward society, he who out of hatred of the wicked breaks the token of that society treads a path that slopes to a fall from the communion of saints. Let them ponder that in a great multitude there are many men, truly holy and innocent in the Lord's sight, who escape their notice. Let them ponder that even among those who seem diseased there are many who in no wise are pleased with, or flatter themselves in, their faults, but aroused again and again by a profound fear of the Lord, aspire to a more upright life. Let them ponder that a man is not to be judged for one deed, inasmuch as the holiest sometimes undergo a most grievous fall. Let them ponder how much more important both the ministry of the Word and participation in the sacred mysteries are for the gathering of the church than the possibility that this whole power may be dissipated through the guilt of certain ungodly men. Finally, let them realize that in estimating the true church divine judgment is of more weight than human.

IV.i.17   The church is holy, then, in the sense that it is daily advancing and is not yet perfect: it makes progress from day to day but has not yet reached its goal of holiness, as will be explained more fully elsewhere. The prophets prophesy that there will be a holy Jerusalem through which "strangers shall never pass" [Joel 3:17], and a most holy temple wherein the unclean shall not enter [Isa. 35:8; cf. ch. 52:1]. Let us not understand this prophecy as if all the members of the church were without blemish; but because they zealously aspire to holiness and perfect purity, the cleanness that they have not yet fully attained is granted them by God's kindness.

IV.i.19   Let the following two points, then, stand firm. First, he who voluntarily deserts the outward communion of the church (where the Word of God is preached and the sacraments are administered) is without excuse. Secondly, neither the vices of the few nor the vices of the many in any way prevent us from duly professing our faith there in ceremonies ordained by God. For a godly conscience is not wounded by the unworthiness of another, whether pastor or layman; nor are the sacraments less pure and salutary for a holy and upright man because they are handled by unclean persons.

2. FUNCTION: THE FORGIVENESS OF SINS

IV.i.20   In the Creed forgiveness of sins appropriately follows mention of the church. For, as one reads in the prophet, only the citizenry and household of the church obtain this [Isa. 33:14–24]. Therefore, the building of the heavenly Jerusalem ought to come first, and in it the kindness of God should then have a place in order that the iniquity of all who come to it may be blotted out. Now I say that it ought first to be built up, not that there can be any church without forgiveness of sins, but because the Lord has promised his mercy solely in the communion of saints.

IV.i.21   Not only does the Lord through forgiveness of sins receive and adopt us once for all into the church, but through the same means he preserves and protects us there. For what would be the point of providing a pardon for us that was destined to be of no use? Every godly man is his own witness that the Lord's mercy, if it were granted only once, would be void and illusory, since each is quite aware throughout his life of the many infirmities that need God's mercy. And clearly not in vain does God promise this grace especially to those of his own household; not in vain does he order the same message of reconciliation daily to be brought to them. So, carrying, as we do, the traces of sin around with us throughout life, unless we are sustained by the Lord's constant grace in forgiving our sins, we shall scarcely abide one moment in the church. But the Lord has called his children to eternal salvation. Therefore, they ought to ponder that there is pardon ever ready for their sins. Consequently, we must firmly believe that by God's generosity, mediated by Christ's merit, through the sanctification of the Spirit, sins have been and are daily pardoned to us who have been received and engrafted into the body of the church.

IV.i.22   We should accordingly note three things here. First, however great the holiness in which God's children excel, they still—so long as they dwell in mortal bodies—remain unable to stand before God without forgiveness of sins. Secondly, this benefit so belongs to the church that we cannot enjoy it unless we abide in communion with the church. Thirdly, it is dispensed to us through the ministers and pastors of the church, either by the preaching of the gospel or by the administration of the sacraments; and herein chiefly stands out the power of the keys, which the Lord has conferred upon the society of believers. Accordingly, let each one of us count it his own duty to seek forgiveness of sins only where the Lord has placed it.

XXII

THE GOVERNMENT
OF THE CHURCH

1. ORDAINED BY GOD

IV.iii.1   Now we must speak of the order by which the Lord
willed his church to be governed. He alone should
rule and reign in the church as well as have authority or pre-
eminence in it, and this authority should be exercised and
administered by his Word alone. Nevertheless, because he
does not dwell among us in visible presence [Matt. 26:11], we
have said that he uses the ministry of men to declare openly
his will to us by mouth, as a sort of delegated work, not by
transferring to them his right and honor, but only that through
their mouths he may do his own work—just as a workman uses
a tool to do his work. . . . For by this means he first declares
his regard for us when from among men he takes some to serve
as his ambassadors in the world [cf. 2 Cor. 5:20], to be interpreters of his secret will and, in short, to represent his person.
And by this evidence he proves it to be no idle speaking that
he often calls us his temples [1 Cor. 3:16–17; 6:19; 2 Cor. 6:16],
since from the lips of men, as from the sanctuary, he gives his
answers to men.

Again, this is the best and most useful exercise in humility,
when he accustoms us to obey his Word, even though it be
preached through men like us and sometimes even by those
of lower worth than we. If he spoke from heaven, it would not
be surprising if his sacred oracles were to be reverently received without delay by the ears and minds of all. For who
would not dread the presence of his power? Who would not be
stricken down at the sight of such great majesty? Who would
not be confounded at such boundless splendor? But when a
puny man risen from the dust speaks in God's name, at this
point we best evidence our piety and obedience toward God

if we show ourselves teachable toward his minister, although he excels us in nothing. It was for this reason, then, that he hid the treasure of his heavenly wisdom in weak and earthen vessels [2 Cor. 4:7] in order to prove more surely how much we should esteem it.

Further, nothing fosters mutual love more fittingly than for men to be bound together with this bond: one is appointed pastor to teach the rest, and those bidden to be pupils receive the common teaching from one mouth. For if anyone were sufficient to himself and needed no one else's help (such is the pride of human nature), each man would despise the rest and be despised by them. The Lord has therefore bound his church together with a knot that he foresaw would be the strongest means of keeping unity, while he entrusted to men the teaching of salvation and everlasting life in order that through their hands it might be communicated to the rest.

IV.iii.2   Whoever, therefore, either is trying to abolish this order of which we speak and this kind of government, or discounts it as not necessary, is striving for the undoing or rather the ruin and destruction of the church. For neither the light and heat of the sun, nor food and drink, are so necessary to nourish and sustain the present life as the apostolic and pastoral office is necessary to preserve the church on earth.

2. THE OFFICERS OF THE CHURCH
AND THEIR DUTIES

IV.iii.4   Those who preside over the government of the church in accordance with Christ's institution are called by Paul as follows: first apostles, then prophets, thirdly evangelists, fourthly pastors, and finally teachers [Eph. 4:11]. Of these only the last two have an ordinary office in the church; the Lord raised up the first three at the beginning of his Kingdom, and now and again revives them as the need of the times demands.

The nature of the apostles' function is clear from this command: "Go, preach the gospel to every creature" [Mark 16:15]. No set limits are allotted to them, but the whole earth is assigned to them to bring into obedience to Christ, in order that by spreading the gospel wherever they can among the nations, they may raise up his Kingdom everywhere. Accordingly, Paul, in desiring to prove his apostleship, recalls that he did not gain any one city for Christ but propagated the gospel far and wide, and did not put his hands to another man's foundation but planted churches where the name of the Lord was unheard [Rom. 15:19–20]. Apostles, then, were sent out to lead the world back from rebellion to true obedience to God, and to establish his Kingdom everywhere by the preaching of the gospel, or, if you prefer, as the first builders of the church, to lay its foundations in all the world [1 Cor. 3:10].

Paul applies the name "prophets" not to all those who were interpreters of God's will, but to those who excelled in a particular revelation [Eph. 4:11]. This class either does not exist today or is less commonly seen.

"Evangelists" I take to be those who, although lower in rank than apostles, were next to them in office and functioned in their place. Such were Luke, Timothy, Titus, and others like them; perhaps also the seventy disciples, whom Christ appointed in the second place after the apostles [Luke 10:1].

According to this interpretation (which seems to me to be in agreement with both the words and opinion of Paul), these three functions were not established in the church as permanent ones, but only for that time during which churches were to be erected where none existed before, or where they were to be carried over from Moses to Christ. Still, I do not deny that the Lord has sometimes at a later period raised up apostles, or at least evangelists in their place, as has happened in our own day. For there was need for such persons to lead the church back from the rebellion of Antichrist. Nonetheless, I call this office "extraordinary," because in duly constituted churches it has no place.

Next come pastors and teachers, whom the church can never go without. There is, I believe, this difference between them: teachers are not put in charge of discipline, or administering the sacraments, or warnings and exhortations, but only of Scriptural interpretation—to keep doctrine whole and pure among believers. But the pastoral office includes all these functions within itself.

IV.iii.5   We have now in mind which ministries in the government of the church were temporary and which ones were so instituted as to endure permanently. But if we group evangelists and apostles together, we shall then have two pairs that somehow correspond with each other. For as our teachers correspond to the ancient prophets, so do our pastors to the apostles.

IV.iii.6   The Lord, when he sent out the apostles, gave them (as has just now been said) the command to preach the gospel and to baptize those who believe unto forgiveness of sins [Matt. 28:19]. But he had previously commanded that they distribute the sacred symbols of his body and blood after his example [Luke 22:19]. Here is the holy, inviolable, and perpetual law imposed upon those who took the place of the apostles, by which they receive the command to preach the gospel and administer the sacraments. From this we infer that those who neglect both of these pretend falsely to be apostles.

But what about the pastors? Paul is speaking not only of himself but of them all when he says, "This is how men should regard us, as ministers of Christ and stewards of the mysteries of God" [1 Cor. 4:1]. Likewise elsewhere: "The bishop must hold to the faithful word, which is, according to the teaching, that he may be able to give instruction in sound doctrine and also to confute those who contradict it" [Titus 1:9]. From these and similar passages which frequently occur, we may infer that in the office of the pastors also there are these two particular functions: to proclaim the gospel and to administer the sacraments. The manner of teaching not only consists in public discourses, but also has to do with private admonitions. So Paul calls the Ephesians to witness that he shrank from nothing that was in their best interest, but warned and taught them publicly and from house to house, testifying, to Jews and Greeks alike, repentance and faith in Christ [Acts 20:20–21]; likewise, a little later, that he did not cease to admonish them one and all with tears [Acts 20:31].

IV.iii.8   But in indiscriminately calling those who rule the church "bishops," "presbyters," "pastors," and "ministers," I did so according to Scriptural usage, which interchanges these terms. . . . Governors [1 Cor. 12:28] were, I believe, elders chosen from the people, who were charged with the censure of morals and the exercise of discipline along with the bishops. For one cannot otherwise interpret his statement, "Let him who rules act with diligence" [Rom. 12:8; cf. Vg.]. Each church, therefore, had from its beginning a senate, chosen from godly, grave, and holy men, which had jurisdiction over the correcting of faults.

IV.iii.9   The care of the poor was entrusted to the deacons. However, two kinds are mentioned in the letter to the Romans: "He that gives, let him do it with simplicity; . . . he

that shows mercy, with cheerfulness" [Rom. 12:8; cf. Vg.].
Since it is certain that Paul is speaking of the public office of
the church, there must have been two distinct grades. Unless
my judgment deceive me, in the first clause he designates the
deacons who distribute the alms. But the second refers to those
who had devoted themselves to the care of the poor and sick.
Of this sort were the widows whom Paul mentions to Timothy
[1 Tim. 5:9–10].

3. THE MINISTRY: ORDINATION AND INDUCTION

IV.iii.10   But while "all things should be done decently and in
             order" [1 Cor. 14:40] in the holy assembly, there is
nothing in which order should be more diligently observed
than in establishing government; for nowhere is there greater
peril if anything be done irregularly. Therefore, in order that
noisy and troublesome men should not rashly take upon themselves to teach or to rule (which might otherwise happen),
especial care was taken that no one should assume public office
in the church without being called. Therefore, if a man were
to be considered a true minister of the church, he must first
have been duly called [Heb. 5:4], then he must respond to his
calling, that is, he must undertake and carry out the tasks
enjoined.

IV.iii.11   The treatment of this matter involves four points: that
             we may know (1) what sort of ministers they should
be, (2) how, and (3) by whom they should be appointed, and
(4) by what rite or ceremony they should be installed. I am
speaking of the outward and solemn call which has to do with
the public order of the church. I pass over that secret call, of
which each minister is conscious before God, and which does
not have the church as witness.

IV.iii.12   In two passages [Titus 1:7; 1 Tim. 3:1–7] Paul fully sets
             forth what sort of bishops ought to be chosen. To sum
up, only those are to be chosen who are of sound doctrine and
of holy life, not notorious in any fault which might both deprive them of authority and disgrace the ministry [1 Tim.
3:2–3; Titus 1:7–8].

IV.iii.13   The third point in our discussion is: who should choose
             the ministers? The election of the apostles provides no

sure rule in this matter, for it was somewhat different from the calling of the rest.

IV.iii.15   Someone now asks whether the minister ought to be chosen by the whole church, or only by his colleagues and the elders charged with the censure of morals, or whether he ought to be appointed by the authority of a single person. . . . We therefore hold that this call of a minister is lawful according to the Word of God, when those who seemed fit are created by the consent and approval of the people; moreover, that other pastors ought to preside over the election in order that the multitude may not go wrong either through fickleness, through evil intentions, or through disorder.

IV.iii.16   There remains the rite of ordination, to which we have given the last place in the call. It is clear that when the apostles admitted any man to the ministry, they used no other ceremony than the laying on of hands. . . .

Although there exists no set precept for the laying on of hands, because we see it in continual use with the apostles, their very careful observance ought to serve in lieu of a precept. And surely it is useful for the dignity of the ministry to be commended to the people by this sort of sign, as also to warn the one ordained that he is no longer a law unto himself, but bound in servitude to God and the church.

XXIII

THE AUTHORITY
OF THE CHURCH

1. DOCTRINE AND THE WORD OF GOD

IV.viii.1   There now follows the third section, on the power of
the church, which resides partly in individual bishops,
and partly in councils, either provincial or general. I speak only
of the spiritual power, which is proper to the church. This,
moreover, consists either in doctrine or in jurisdiction or in
making laws. The doctrinal side has two parts: authority to lay
down articles of faith, and authority to explain them. . . .

Now the only way to build up the church is for the ministers
themselves to endeavor to preserve Christ's authority for himself; this can only be secured if what he has received from his
Father be left to him, namely, that he alone is the schoolmaster
of the church. For it is written not of any other but of him
alone, "Hear him" [Matt. 17:5]. The power of the church is
therefore to be not grudgingly manifested but yet to be kept
within definite limits, that it may not be drawn hither and
thither according to men's whim.

IV.viii.2   Accordingly, we must here remember that whatever
authority and dignity the Spirit in Scripture accords
to either priests or prophets, or apostles, or successors of apostles, it is wholly given not to the men personally, but to the
ministry to which they have been appointed; or (to speak more
briefly) to the Word, whose ministry is entrusted to them. For
if we examine them all in order, we shall not find that they
have been endowed with any authority to teach or to answer,
except in the name and Word of the Lord. For, where they are
called to office, it is at the same time enjoined upon them not
to bring anything of themselves, but to speak from the Lord's
mouth. And he himself does not bring them forth to be heard

by the people before teaching them what to speak: they are to speak nothing but his Word.

IV.viii.5   But although this principle has prevailed in the church from the beginning and ought to prevail today, that the servants of God should teach nothing which they have not learned from him, still, according to the diversity of the times, they have had divers ways of learning. But the present order differs very much from what existed in former times. First, if what Christ says is true—"No one sees the Father except the Son and anyone to whom the Son chooses to reveal him" [Matt. 11:27]—surely they who would attain the knowledge of God should always be directed by that eternal Wisdom. For how could they either have comprehended God's mysteries with the mind, or have uttered them, except by the teaching of him to whom alone the secrets of the Father are revealed? . . .

For this Wisdom has not always manifested itself in one way. Among the patriarchs God used secret revelations, but at the same time to confirm these he added such signs that they could have no doubt that it was God who was speaking to them. What the patriarchs had received they handed on to their descendants. For the Lord had left it with them on this condition, that they should so propagate it. The children and children's children knew when God dictates within that what they heard was from heaven, not from earth.

IV.viii.6   But where it pleased God to raise up a more visible form of the church, he willed to have his Word set down and sealed in writing, that his priests might seek from it what to teach the people, and that every doctrine to be taught should conform to that rule. Therefore, after the law has been published, the priests are bidden to teach "from the mouth of the Lord" [Mal. 2:7; cf. Vg. and Comm.]. This means that they should teach nothing strange or foreign to that doctrine which God included in the law; indeed, it was unlawful for them to add to it or take away from it [Deut. 4:2; 13:1].

There then followed the prophets, through whom God published new oracles which were added to the law—but not so new that they did not flow from the law and hark back to it. As for doctrine, they were only interpreters of the law and added nothing to it except predictions of things to come. Apart from these, they brought nothing forth but a pure exposition of the law. But because the Lord was pleased to reveal a clearer and fuller doctrine in order better to satisfy weak consciences, he commanded that the prophecies also be committed to writing and be accounted part of his Word. At the same time, histories were added to these, also the labor of the prophets, but composed under the Holy Spirit's dictation. I include the psalms with the prophecies, since what we attribute to the prophecies is common to them.

Therefore, that whole body, put together out of law, prophecies, psalms, and histories, was the Lord's Word for the ancient people; and to this standard, priests and teachers, even to the coming of Christ, had to conform their teaching. And it was not lawful for them to turn aside either to the right or to the left [Deut. 5:32], for their whole office was limited to answering the people from the mouth of God.

IV.viii.7   But when the Wisdom of God was at length revealed in the flesh, that Wisdom heartily declared to us all that can be comprehended and ought to be pondered concerning the Heavenly Father by the human mind. Now therefore, since Christ, the Sun of Righteousness, has shone, while before there was only dim light, we have the perfect radiance of divine truth, like the wonted brilliance of midday. For truly the apostle meant to proclaim no common thing when he wrote, "In many and various ways God spoke of old to the fathers by the prophets; but in these last days he has begun to speak to us through his beloved Son" [Heb. 1:1–2 p; cf. Comm.]. For Paul means, in fact, openly declares, that God will not speak hereafter as he did before, intermittently through some and through others; nor will he add prophecies to prophecies, or revelations to revelations. Rather, he has so fulfilled all functions of teaching in his Son that we must regard this as the final and eternal testimony from him. In this way this whole New Testament time, from the point that Christ appeared to us with the preaching of his gospel even to the Day of Judgment, is designated by "the last hour" [1 John 2:18], "the last times" [1 Tim. 4:1; 1 Peter 1:20], "the last days" [Acts 2:17; 2 Tim. 3:1; 2 Peter 3:3]. This is done that, content with the perfection of Christ's teaching, we may learn not to fashion anything new for ourselves beyond this or to admit anything contrived by others.

It was therefore with good reason that the Father by a singular privilege ordained the Son as our teacher, commanding him, and not any man, to be heard. He has, indeed, in few words commended Christ as our teacher when he says, "Hear him" [Matt. 17:5]. But in these words there is more weight and force than is commonly thought. For it is as if, leading us away from all doctrines of men, he should conduct us to his Son alone; bid us seek all teaching of salvation from him alone; depend upon him, cleave to him; in short (as the words themselves pronounce), hearken to his voice alone. And what, indeed, ought we now either to expect or to hope from man, when the very Word of life has intimately and openly disclosed himself to us? But the mouths of all men should be closed when once he has spoken, in whom the Heavenly Father willed all the treasures of knowledge and wisdom to be hid [Col. 2:3], and has, indeed, so spoken as befitted the wisdom of God (which is in every part seamless [cf. John 19:23]) and the Messiah (from whom the revelation of all things was awaited [John 4:25]); that is, after himself he left nothing for others to say.

IV.viii.8   Let this be a firm principle: No other word is to be held as the Word of God, and given place as such in the church, than what is contained first in the Law and the Prophets, then in the writings of the apostles; and the only authorized way of teaching in the church is by the prescription and standard of his Word.

IV.viii.9   Here, then, is the sovereign power with which the pastors of the church, by whatever name they be called, ought to be endowed. That is that they may dare boldly to do all things by God's Word; may compel all worldly power, glory, wisdom, and exaltation to yield to and obey his majesty; supported by his power, may command all from the highest even to the last; may build up Christ's household and cast down Satan's; may feed the sheep and drive away the wolves; may instruct and exhort the teachable; may accuse, rebuke, and subdue the rebellious and stubborn: may bind and loose; finally, if need be, may launch thunderbolts and lightnings; but do all things in God's Word.

Yet this, as I have said, is the difference between the apostles and their successors: the former were sure and genuine scribes of the Holy Spirit, and their writings are therefore to be considered oracles of God; but the sole office of others is to teach what is provided and sealed in the Holy Scriptures. We therefore teach that faithful ministers are now not permitted to coin any new doctrine, but that they are simply to cleave to that doctrine to which God has subjected all men without exception. When I say this, I mean to show what is permitted not only to individual men but to the whole church as well.

2. THE LAW OF GOD AND HUMAN LAW

IV.x.27   Many unlettered persons, when they are told that men's consciences are impiously bound by human traditions, and God is worshiped in vain, apply the same erasure to all the laws by which the order of the church is shaped. It is convenient here to deal also with their error. At this point it is exceedingly easy to be deceived, for it is not apparent at first sight how much difference there is between the former and the latter sort of regulations. I shall briefly explain the whole matter so clearly that no one will be deceived by the similarity.

First, let us grasp this consideration. We see that some form of organization is necessary in all human society to foster the common peace and maintain concord. We further see that in human transactions some procedure is always in effect, which is to be respected in the interests of public decency, and even of humanity itself. This ought especially to be observed in churches, which are best sustained when all things are under a well-ordered constitution, and which without concord become no churches at all. Therefore, if we wish to provide for the safety of the church, we must attend with all diligence to Paul's command that "all things be done decently and in order" [1 Cor. 14:40].

Yet since such diversity exists in the customs of men, such variety in their minds, such conflicts in their judgments and dispositions, no organization is sufficiently strong unless constituted with definite laws; nor can any procedure be maintained without some set form. Therefore, we are so far from condemning the laws that conduce to this as to contend that, when churches are deprived of them, their very sinews disintegrate and they are wholly deformed and scattered. Nor can Paul's requirement—that "all things be done decently and in order"—be met unless order itself and decorum be established through the addition of observances that form, as it were, a bond of union. But in these observances one thing must be guarded against. They are not to be considered necessary for salvation and thus bind consciences by scruples; nor are they to be associated with the worship of God, and piety thus be lodged in them.

IV.x.28   We therefore have a most excellent and dependable mark to distinguish between those impious constitutions (which, as we have said, obscure true religion and subvert consciences) and legitimate church observances. We have this if we remember that the end in view must always be one of two things, or both together—that in the sacred assembly of believers all things be done decently and with becoming dignity; and that the human community itself be kept in order with certain bonds of humanity and moderation. For when it is once understood that a law has been made for the sake of public decency, there is taken away the superstition into which those fall who measure the worship of God by human inventions. Again, when it is recognized that the law has to do with common usage, then that false opinion of obligation and necessity, which struck consciences with great terror when traditions were thought necessary to salvation, is overthrown. For here nothing is required except that love be fostered among us by common effort.

But it is worthwhile to define still more clearly what is included under that decorum which Paul commends, and also under order [1 Cor. 14:40]. The purpose of decorum is in part that, when rites are used which promote reverence toward sacred things, we be aroused to piety by such aids; in part, also, that modesty and gravity, which ought to be seen in all honorable acts, may greatly shine there. The first point in order is that those in charge know the rule and law of good governing, but that the people who are governed become accustomed to obedience to God and to right discipline. The second point is, when we have the church set up in good order, we provide for its peace and quietness.

IV.x.30   I approve only those human constitutions which are founded upon God's authority, drawn from Scripture, and, therefore, wholly divine. Let us take, for example, kneeling when solemn prayers are being said. The question is whether it is a human tradition, which any man may lawfully repudiate or neglect. I say that it is human, as it is also divine. It is of God in so far as it is a part of that decorum whose care and observance the apostle has commended to us [1 Cor. 14:40]. But it is of men in so far as it specifically designates what had in general been suggested rather than explicitly stated.

By this one example we may judge what opinion we should have of this whole class. I mean that the Lord has in his sacred oracles faithfully embraced and clearly expressed both the whole sum of true righteousness, and all aspects of the worship of his majesty, and whatever was necessary to salvation; therefore, in these the Master alone is to be heard. But because he did not will in outward discipline and ceremonies to prescribe in detail what we ought to do (because he foresaw that this depended upon the state of the times, and he did not deem one form suitable for all ages), here we must take refuge in those general rules which he has given, that whatever the necessity of the church will require for order and decorum should be tested against these. Lastly, because he has taught nothing specifically, and because these things are not necessary to salvation, and for the upbuilding of the church ought to be variously accommodated to the customs of each nation and age, it will be fitting (as the advantage of the church will require) to change and abrogate traditional practices and to establish new ones. Indeed, I admit that we ought not to charge into innovation rashly, suddenly, for insufficient cause. But love will best judge what may hurt or edify; and if we let love be our guide, all will be safe.

IV.x.31   Now it is the duty of Christian people to keep the ordinances that have been established according to this rule with a free conscience, indeed, without superstition, yet with a pious and ready inclination to obey; not to despise them, not to pass over them in careless negligence. So far ought we to be from openly violating them through pride and obstinacy!

What sort of freedom of conscience could there be in such excessive attentiveness and caution? Indeed, it will be very clear when we consider that these are no fixed and permanent sanctions by which we are bound, but outward rudiments for human weakness. Although not all of us need them, we all use them, for we are mutually bound, one to another, to nourish mutual love. This may be recognized in the examples set forth above. What? Does religion consist in a woman's shawl, so that it is unlawful for her to go out with a bare head? Is that decree of Paul's concerning silence so holy that it cannot be broken without great offense? Is there in bending the knee or in burying a corpse any holy rite that cannot be neglected without offense? Not at all. For if a woman needs such haste to help a neighbor that she cannot stop to cover her head, she does not offend if she runs to her with head uncovered. And there is a place where it is no less proper for her to speak than elsewhere to remain silent. Also, nothing prohibits a man who cannot bend his knees because of disease from standing to pray. Finally, it is better to bury a dead man in due time than, where a shroud is lacking, or where there are no pallbearers to carry him, to wait until the unburied corpse decays. Nevertheless, the established custom of the region, or humanity itself and the rule of modesty, dictate what is to be done or avoided in these matters. In them a man commits no crime if out of imprudence or forgetfulness he departs from them; but if out of contempt, this willfulness is to be disapproved. Similarly, the days themselves, the hours, the structure of the places of worship, what psalms are to be sung on what day, are matters of no importance. But it is convenient to have definite days and stated hours, and a place suitable to receive all, if there is any concern for the preservation of peace.

3. THE SPIRITUAL JURISDICTION OF THE CHURCH

IV vi.1 There remains the third part of ecclesiastical power, the most important in a well-ordered state. This, as we have said, consists in jurisdiction. . . . For as no city or township can function without magistrate and polity, so the church of God (as I have already taught, but am now compelled to repeat) needs a spiritual polity. This is, however, quite distinct from the civil polity, yet does not hinder or threaten it but rather greatly helps and furthers it. Therefore, this power of jurisdiction will be nothing, in short, but an order framed for the preservation of the spiritual polity. For this purpose courts of judgment were established in the church from the beginning to deal with the censure of morals, to investigate vices, and to be charged with the exercise of the office of the keys.

IV.xi.3 The church does not have the right of the sword to punish or compel, not the authority to force; not imprisonment, nor the other punishments which the magistrate commonly inflicts. Then, it is not a question of punishing the sinner against his will, but of the sinner professing his repentance in a voluntary chastisement. The two conceptions are very different. The church does not assume what is proper to the magistrate; nor can the magistrate execute what is carried out by the church. . . . As the magistrate ought by punishment and physical restraint to cleanse the church of offenses, so the minister of the Word in turn ought to help the magistrate in order that not so many may sin. Their functions ought to be so joined that each serves to help, not hinder, the other.

4. THE MAINTENANCE OF DISCIPLINE

IV.xii.1 Discipline depends for the most part upon the power of the keys and upon spiritual jurisdiction. To understand it better, let us divide the church into two chief orders: clergy and people. I call by the usual name "clergy" those who perform the public ministry in the church. We shall first speak of common discipline, to which all ought to submit; then we shall come to the clergy, who, besides the common discipline, have their own.

But because some persons, in their hatred of discipline, recoil from its very name, let them understand this: if no society, indeed, no house which has even a small family, can be kept in proper condition without discipline, it is much more necessary in the church, whose condition should be as ordered as possible. Accordingly, as the saving doctrine of Christ is the soul of the church, so does discipline serve as its sinews, through which the members of the body hold together, each in its own place. Therefore, all who desire to remove discipline or to hinder its restoration—whether they do this deliberately or out of ignorance—are surely contributing to the ultimate dissolution of the church. For what will happen if each is allowed to do what he pleases? Yet that would happen, if to the preaching of doctrine there were not added private admonitions, corrections, and other aids of the sort that sustain doctrine and do not let it remain idle. Therefore, discipline is like a bridle to restrain and tame those who rage against the doctrine of Christ; or like a spur to arouse those of little inclination; and also sometimes like a father's rod to chastise mildly and with the gentleness of Christ's Spirit those who have more seriously lapsed.

IV.xii.2   The first foundation of discipline is to provide a place for private admonition; that is, if anyone does not perform his duty willingly, or behaves insolently, or does not live honorably, or has committed any act deserving blame—he should allow himself to be admonished; and when the situation demands it, every man should endeavor to admonish his brother. But let pastors and presbyters be especially watchful to do this, for their duty is not only to preach to the people, but to warn and exhort in every house, wherever they are not effective enough in general instruction.

IV.xii.6   It remains for us to see how the church carries out this part of discipline which falls within its jurisdiction. To begin with, let us keep the division set forth above: that some sins are public; others, private or somewhat secret. Public sins are those witnessed not by one or two persons, but committed openly and to the offense of the entire church. I call secret sins, not those completely hidden from men, as are those of hypocrites (for these do not fall under the judgment of the church), but those of an intermediate sort, which are not unwitnessed, yet not public.

The first kind does not require the steps which Christ lists [Matt. 18:15-17]; but when any such sin appears, the church ought to do its duty in summoning the sinner and correcting him according to his fault. In the second kind, according to that rule of Christ, the case does not come before the church until the sinner becomes obstinate. When it has come before the church, then the other division between crimes and faults is to be observed. For such great severity is not to be used in lighter sins, but verbal chastisement is enough—and that mild and fatherly—which should not harden or confuse the sinner, but bring him back to himself, that he may rejoice rather than be sad that he has been corrected. But shameful acts need to be chastised with a harsher remedy. Nor is it enough if he, who by setting a bad example through his misdeed has gravely injured the church, be chastised only with words; but he ought for a time to be deprived of the communion of the Supper until he gives assurance of his repentance.

XXIV

THE SACRAMENTS

1. THE NATURE AND PURPOSE
OF THE SACRAMENTS

IV.xiv.1   We have in the sacraments another aid to our faith related to the preaching of the gospel. It is very important that some definite doctrine concerning them be taught, that we may learn from it both the purpose for which they were instituted and their present use.

First, we must consider what a sacrament is. It seems to me that a simple and proper definition would be to say that it is an outward sign by which the Lord seals on our consciences the promises of his good will toward us in order to sustain the weakness of our faith; and we in turn attest our piety toward him in the presence of the Lord and of his angels and before men. Here is another briefer definition: one may call it a testimony of divine grace toward us, confirmed by an outward sign, with mutual attestation of our piety toward him. Whichever of these definitions you may choose, it does not differ in meaning from that of Augustine, who teaches that a sacrament is "a visible sign of a sacred thing," or "a visible form of an invisible grace."

IV.xiv.3   A sacrament is never without a preceding promise but is joined to it as a sort of appendix, with the purpose of confirming and sealing the promise itself, and of making it more evident to us and in a sense ratifying it. By this means God provides first for our ignorance and dullness, then for our weakness. Yet, properly speaking, it is not so much needed to confirm his Sacred Word as to establish us in faith in it. For God's truth is of itself firm and sure enough, and it cannot receive better confirmation from any other source than from itself. But as our faith is slight and feeble unless it be propped on all sides and sustained by every means, it trembles, wavers, totters, and at last gives way. Here our merciful Lord, according to his infinite kindness, so tempers himself to our capacity that, since we are creatures who always creep on the ground, cleave to the flesh, and do not think about or even conceive of anything spiritual, he condescends to lead us to himself even by these earthly elements, and to set before us in the flesh a mirror of spiritual blessings.

IV.xiv.9   The sacraments properly fulfill their office only when the Spirit, that inward teacher, comes to them, by whose power alone hearts are penetrated and affections moved and our souls opened for the sacraments to enter in. If the Spirit be lacking, the sacraments can accomplish nothing more in our minds than the splendor of the sun shining upon blind eyes, or a voice sounding in deaf ears. Therefore, I make such a division between Spirit and sacraments that the power to act rests with the former, and the ministry alone is left to the latter—a ministry empty and trifling, apart from the action of the Spirit, but charged with great effect when the Spirit works within and manifests his power.

Now it is clear in what way, according to this opinion, the godly mind is strengthened in faith through the sacraments. That is, just as the eyes see by the brightness of the sun, or the ears hear by the sound of a voice, so the eyes would not be affected by any light unless they were endowed with a sharpness of vision capable of being illumined of themselves; and the ears would never be struck by any noise, unless they were created and fitted for hearing. But suppose it is true (something that ought at once to be clear among us) that what sight does in our eyes for seeing light, and what hearing does in our ears for perceiving a voice, are analogous to the work of the Holy Spirit in our hearts, which is to conceive, sustain, nourish, and establish faith. Then both of these things follow: the sacraments profit not a whit without the power of the Holy Spirit, and nothing prevents them from strengthening and enlarging faith in hearts already taught by that Schoolmaster. There is only this difference: that our ears and eyes have naturally received the faculty of hearing and seeing; but Christ does the same thing in our hearts by special grace beyond the measure of nature.

IV.xiv.17   Let it be regarded as a settled principle that the sacraments have the same office as the Word of God: to offer and set forth Christ to us, and in him the treasures of heavenly grace. But they avail and profit nothing unless received in faith. As with wine or oil or some other liquid, no matter how much you pour out, it will flow away and disappear unless the mouth of the vessel to receive it is open; moreover, the vessel will be splashed over on the outside, but will still remain void and empty. . . .

The sacraments . . . are for us the same thing from God, as messengers of glad tidings or guarantees of the ratification of covenants are from men. They do not bestow any grace of themselves, but announce and tell us, and (as they are guarantees and tokens) ratify among us, those things given us by divine bounty. The Holy Spirit (whom the sacraments do not bring indiscriminately to all men but whom the Lord exclusively bestows on his own people) is he who brings the graces of God with him, gives a place for the sacraments among us, and makes them bear fruit.

IV.xiv.20 The sacraments themselves were also diverse, in keeping with the times, according to the dispensation by which the Lord was pleased to reveal himself in various ways to men. For circumcision was enjoined upon Abraham and his descendants [Gen. 17:10]. To it were afterward added purifications [Lev., chs. 11 to 15], sacrifices, and other rites [Lev., chs. 1 to 10] from the law of Moses. These were the sacraments of the Jews until the coming of Christ. When at his coming these were abrogated, two sacraments were instituted which the Christian church now uses, Baptism and the Lord's Supper [Matt. 26:26–28; 28:19]. . . .

Yet those ancient sacraments looked to the same purpose to which ours now tend: to direct and almost lead men by the hand to Christ, or rather, as images, to represent him and show him forth to be known. We have already taught that they are seals by which God's promises are sealed, and, moreover, it is very clear that no promise has ever been offered to men except in Christ [2 Cor. 1:20]. Consequently, to teach us about any promise of God, they must show forth Christ. To this pertains that heavenly pattern of the Tabernacle and of worship under the law, which was put before Moses on the mountain [Ex. 25:9, 40; 26:30]. There is only one difference: the former foreshadowed Christ promised while he was as yet awaited; the latter attest him as already given and revealed.

IV.xiv.22 As for our sacraments, the more fully Christ has been revealed to men, the more clearly do the sacraments present him to us from the time when he was truly revealed by the Father as he had been promised. For baptism attests to us that we have been cleansed and washed; the Eucharistic Supper, that we have been redeemed. In water, washing is represented; in blood, satisfaction. These two are found in Christ, "who," as John says, "came in water and blood" [1 John 5:6]; that is, to wash and to redeem. The Spirit of God is also witness of this. Indeed, "there are three witnesses in one: the water, the blood, and the Spirit" [1 John 5:8 p]. In the water and the blood we have testimony of cleansing and redemption. But the Spirit, the primary witness, makes us certain of such testimony. This lofty mystery has been admirably shown us in the cross of Christ, when water and blood flowed from his sacred side [John 19:34].

2. BAPTISM

IV.xv.1   Baptism is the sign of the initiation by which we are received into the society of the church, in order that, engrafted in Christ, we may be reckoned among God's children. Now baptism was given to us by God for these ends (which I have taught to be common to all sacraments): first, to serve our faith before him; secondly, to serve our confession before men. We shall treat in order the reasons for each aspect of its institution. Baptism brings three things to our faith which we must deal with individually. The first thing that the Lord sets out for us is that baptism should be a token and proof of our cleansing; or (the better to explain what I mean) it is like a sealed document to confirm to us that all our sins are so abolished, remitted, and effaced that they can never come to his sight, be recalled, or charged against us. For he wills that all who believe be baptized for the remission of sins [Matt. 28:19; Acts 2:38].

Accordingly, they who regarded baptism as nothing but a token and mark by which we confess our religion before men, as soldiers bear the insignia of their commander as a mark of their profession, have not weighed what was the chief point of baptism. It is to receive baptism with this promise: "He who believes and is baptized will be saved" [Mark 16:16].

IV.xv.2   Baptism promises us no other purification than through the sprinkling of Christ's blood, which is represented by means of water from the resemblance to cleansing and washing. Who, therefore, may say that we are cleansed by this water which attests with certainty that Christ's blood is our true and only laver? Thus, the surest argument to refute the self-deception of those who attribute everything to the power of the water can be sought in the meaning of baptism itself, which draws us away, not only from the visible element which meets our eyes, but from all other means, that it may fasten our minds upon Christ alone.

IV.xv.3   But we are not to think that baptism was conferred upon us only for past time, so that for newly committed sins into which we fall after baptism we must seek new remedies of expiation in some other sacraments, as if the force of the former one were spent. In early times this error caused some to refuse the initiation by baptism unless in uttermost peril of life and at their last gasp, so that thus they might obtain pardon for their whole life. The ancient bishops frequently inveighed in their writings against this preposterous caution. But we must realize that at whatever time we are baptized, we are once for all washed and purged for our whole life. Therefore, as often as we fall away, we ought to recall the memory of our baptism and fortify our mind with it, that we may always be sure and confident of the forgiveness of sins. For, though baptism, administered only once, seemed to have passed, it was still not destroyed by subsequent sins. For Christ's purity has been offered us in it; his purity ever flourishes; it is defiled by no spots, but buries and cleanses away all our defilements.

Nevertheless, from this fact we ought not to take leave to sin in the future, as this has certainly not taught us to be so bold. Rather, this doctrine is only given to sinners who groan, wearied and oppressed by their own sins, in order that they may have something to lift them up and comfort them, so as not to plunge into confusion and despair.

IV.xv.5   Baptism also brings another benefit, for it shows us our mortification in Christ, and new life in him. Indeed (as the apostle says), "we have been baptized into his death," "buried with him into death, . . . that we may walk in newness of life" [Rom. 6:3–4 p]. By these words he not only exhorts us to follow Christ as if he had said that we are admonished through baptism to die to our desires by an example of Christ's death, and to be aroused to righteousness by the example of his resurrection. But he also takes hold of something far higher, namely, that through baptism Christ makes us sharers in his death, that we may be engrafted in it [Rom. 6:5; cf. Vg.].... Thus, the free pardon of sins and the imputation of righteousness are first promised us, and then the grace of the Holy Spirit to reform us to newness of life.

IV.xv.6 Lastly, our faith receives from baptism the advantage of its sure testimony to us that we are not only engrafted into the death and life of Christ, but so united to Christ himself that we become sharers in all his blessings. For he dedicated and sanctified baptism in his own body [Matt. 3:13] in order that he might have it in common with us as the firmest bond of the union and fellowship which he has deigned to form with us. Hence, Paul proves that we are children of God from the fact that we put on Christ in baptism [Gal. 3:26–27]. Thus we see that the fulfillment of baptism is in Christ, whom also for this reason we call the proper object of baptism. Consequently, it is not strange that the apostles are reported to have baptized in his name [Acts 8:16; 19:5], although they had also been bidden to baptize in the name of the Father and of the Spirit [Matt. 28:19]. For all the gifts of God proffered in baptism are found in Christ alone. Yet this cannot take place unless he who baptizes in Christ invokes also the names of the Father and the Spirit. For we are cleansed by his blood because our merciful Father, wishing to receive us into grace in accordance with his incomparable kindness, has set this Mediator among us to gain favor for us in his sight. But we obtain regeneration by Christ's death and resurrection only if we are sanctified by the Spirit and imbued with a new and spiritual nature. For this reason we obtain and, so to speak, clearly discern in the Father the cause, in the Son the matter, and in the Spirit the effect, of our purgation and our regeneration.

IV.xv.10 Now, it is clear how false is the teaching, long propagated by some and still persisted in by others, that through baptism we are released and made exempt from original sin, and from the corruption that descended from Adam into all his posterity; and are restored into that same righteousness and purity of nature which Adam would have obtained if he had remained upright as he was first created. For teachers of this type never understood what original sin, what original righteousness, or what the grace of baptism was. But we have already contended that original sin is the depravity and corruption of our nature, which first renders us liable to God's wrath, then also gives rise to what Scripture calls "works of the flesh" [Gal. 5:19]. We must therefore carefully note these two points.

As we are vitiated and corrupted in all parts of our nature, we are held rightly condemned on account of such corruption alone and convicted before God, to whom nothing is acceptable but righteousness, innocence, and purity. Even infants bear their condemnation with them from their mother's womb; for, though they have not yet brought forth the fruits of their own iniquity, they have the seed enclosed within themselves. Indeed, their whole nature is a seed of sin; thus it cannot but be hateful and abominable to God. Through baptism, believers are assured that this condemnation has been removed and withdrawn from them, since (as was said) the Lord promises us by this sign that full and complete remission has been made, both of the guilt that should have been imputed to us, and of the punishment that we ought to have undergone because of the guilt. They also lay hold on righteousness, but such righteousness as the people of God can obtain in this life, that is, by imputation only, since the Lord of his own mercy considers them righteous and innocent.

IV.xv.13   Baptism serves as our confession before men. Indeed, it is the mark by which we publicly profess that we wish to be reckoned God's people; by which we testify that we agree in worshiping the same God, in one religion with all Christians; by which finally we openly affirm our faith. Thus not only do our hearts breathe the praise of God, but our tongues also and all members of our body resound his praise in every way they can. For thus, as is fitting, all our faculties are employed to serve God's glory, which ought to lack nothing, and by our example others are aroused to the same efforts. Paul had this in mind when he asked the Corinthians whether they had not been baptized in Christ's name [1 Cor. 1:13]. He thus implied that, in being baptized in his name, they had devoted themselves to him, sworn allegiance to his name, and pledged their faith to him before men. As a result, they could no longer confess any other but Christ alone, unless they chose to renounce the confession they had made in baptism.

IV.xv.15   From this sacrament, as from all others, we obtain only as much as we receive in faith. If we lack faith, this will be evidence of our ungratefulness, which renders us chargeable before God, because we have not believed the promise given there. But as far as it is a symbol of our confession, we ought by it to testify that our confidence is in God's mercy, and our purity in forgiveness of sins, which has been procured for us through Jesus Christ; and that we enter God's church in order to live harmoniously with all believers in complete agreement of faith and love. This last point was what Paul meant when he said, "We have all been baptized in one Spirit that we may be one body" [1 Cor. 12:13 p].

IV.xv.19 How much better it would be to omit from baptism all theatrical pomp, which dazzles the eyes of the simple and deadens their minds; whenever anyone is to be baptized, to present him to the assembly of believers and, with the whole church looking on as witness and praying over him, offer him to God; to recite the confession of faith with which the catechumen should be instructed; to recount the promises to be had in baptism; to baptize the catechumen in the name of the Father and of the Son and of the Holy Spirit [Matt. 28:19]; lastly, to dismiss him with prayers and thanksgiving. If this were done, nothing essential would be omitted; and that one ceremony, which came from God, its author, not buried in outlandish pollutions, would shine in its full brightness.

But whether the person being baptized should be wholly immersed, and whether thrice or once, whether he should only be sprinkled with poured water—these details are of no importance, but ought to be optional to churches according to the diversity of countries. Yet the word "baptize" means to immerse, and it is clear that the rite of immersion was observed in the ancient church.

IV.xv.22 Infants are not barred from the Kingdom of Heaven just because they happen to depart the present life before they have been immersed in water. Yet . . . serious injustice is done to God's covenant if we do not assent to it, as if it were weak of itself, since its effect depends neither upon baptism nor upon any additions. Afterward, a sort of seal is added to the sacrament, not to confer efficacy upon God's promise as if it were invalid of itself, but only to confirm it to us. From this it follows that the children of believers are baptized not in order that they who were previously strangers to the church may then for the first time become children of God, but rather that, because by the blessing of the promise they already belonged to the body of Christ, they are received into the church with this solemn sign.

Accordingly, if, when the sign is omitted, this is neither from sloth nor contempt nor negligence, we are safe from all danger. It is, therefore, much more holy to revere God's ordinance, namely, that we should seek the sacraments from those only to whom the Lord has committed them. When we cannot receive them from the church, the grace of God is not so bound to them but that we may obtain it by faith from the Word of the Lord.

3. THE LORD'S SUPPER

IV.xvii.1   God has received us, once for all, into his family, to hold us not only as servants but as sons. Thereafter, to fulfill the duties of a most excellent Father concerned for his offspring, he undertakes also to nourish us throughout the course of our life. And not content with this alone, he has willed, by giving his pledge, to assure us of this continuing liberality. To this end, therefore, he has, through the hand of his only-begotten Son, given to his church another sacrament, that is, a spiritual banquet, wherein Christ attests himself to be the life-giving bread, upon which our souls feed unto true and blessed immortality [John 6:51]. . . .

The signs are bread and wine, which represent for us the invisible food that we receive from the flesh and blood of Christ. For as in baptism, God, regenerating us, engrafts us into the society of his church and makes us his own by adoption, so we have said, that he discharges the function of a provident householder in continually supplying to us the food to sustain and preserve us in that life into which he has begotten us by his Word.

Now Christ is the only food of our soul, and therefore our Heavenly Father invites us to Christ, that, refreshed by partaking of him, we may repeatedly gather strength until we shall have reached heavenly immortality.

Since, however, this mystery of Christ's secret union with the devout is by nature incomprehensible, he shows its figure and image in visible signs best adapted to our small capacity. Indeed, by giving guarantees and tokens he makes it as certain for us as if we had seen it with our own eyes. For this very familiar comparison penetrates into even the dullest minds: just as bread and wine sustain physical life, so are souls fed by Christ. We now understand the purpose of this mystical blessing, namely, to confirm for us the fact that the Lord's body was once for all so sacrificed for us that we may now feed upon it, and by feeding feel in ourselves the working of that unique sacrifice; and that his blood was once so shed for us in order to be our perpetual drink. And so speak the words of the promise added there: "Take, this is my body which is given for you" [1 Cor. 11:24; cf. Matt. 26:26; Mark 14:22; Luke 22:19]. We are therefore bidden to take and eat the body which was once for all offered for our salvation, in order that when we see our-selves made partakers in it, we may assuredly conclude that the power of his life-giving death will be efficacious in us. Hence, he also calls the cup "the covenant in his blood" [Luke 22:20; 1 Cor. 11:25]. For he in some measure renews, or rather continues, the covenant which he once for all ratified with his blood (as far as it pertains to the strengthening of our faith) whenever he proffers that sacred blood for us to taste.

IV.xvii.2   Godly souls can gather great assurance and delight from this Sacrament; in it they have a witness of our growth into one body with Christ such that whatever is his may be called ours. As a consequence, we may dare assure ourselves that eternal life, of which he is the heir, is ours; and that the Kingdom of Heaven, into which he has already entered, can no more be cut off from us than from him; again, that we cannot be condemned for our sins, from whose guilt he has absolved us, since he willed to take them upon himself as if they were his own. This is the wonderful exchange which, out of his measureless benevolence, he has made with us; that, becoming Son of man with us, he has made us sons of God with him; that, by his descent to earth, he has prepared an ascent to heaven for us; that, by taking on our mortality, he has con-ferred his immortality upon us; that, accepting our weakness, he has strengthened us by his power; that, receiving our pov-erty unto himself, he has transferred his wealth to us; that, taking the weight of our iniquity upon himself (which op-pressed us), he has clothed us with his righteousness.

IV.xvii.3   In this Sacrament we have such full witness of all these things that we must certainly consider them as if Christ here present were himself set before our eyes and touched by our hands. For his word cannot lie or deceive us: "Take, eat, drink: this is my body, which is given for you; this is my blood, which is shed for forgiveness of sins" [Matt. 26:26–28, conflated with 1 Cor. 11:24; cf. Mark 14:22–24; Luke 22:19–20]. By bidding us take, he indicates that it is ours; by bidding us eat, that it is made one substance with us; by declaring that his body is given for us and his blood shed for us, he teaches that both are not so much his as ours. For he took up and laid down both, not for his own advantage but for our salvation.

And, indeed, we must carefully observe that the very power-ful and almost entire force of the Sacrament lies in these words: "which is given for you," "which is shed for you." The present distribution of the body and blood of the Lord would not greatly benefit us unless they had once for all been given for our redemption and salvation. They are therefore represented under bread and wine so that we may learn not only that they are ours but that they have been destined as food for our spiritual life.

And so as we previously stated, from the physical things set forth in the Sacrament we are led by a sort of analogy to spiritual things. Thus, when bread is given as a symbol of Christ's body, we must at once grasp this comparison: as bread nourishes, sustains, and keeps the life of our body, so Christ's body is the only food to invigorate and enliven our soul. When we see wine set forth as a symbol of blood, we must reflect on the benefits which wine imparts to the body, and so realize that the same are spiritually imparted to us by Christ's blood. These benefits are to nourish, refresh, strengthen, and gladden. For if we sufficiently consider what value we have received from the giving of that most holy body and the shedding of that blood, we shall clearly perceive that those qualities of bread and wine are, according to such an analogy, excellently adapted to express those things when they are communicated to us.

IV.xvii.5 The Sacrament does not cause Christ to begin to be the bread of life; but when it reminds us that he was made the bread of life, which we continually eat, and which gives us a relish and savor of that bread, it causes us to feel the power of that bread. For it assures us that all that Christ did or suffered was done to quicken us; and again, that this quickening is eternal, we being ceaselessly nourished, sustained, and preserved throughout life by it. . . . Once for all, therefore, he gave his body to be made bread when he yielded himself to be crucified for the redemption of the world; daily he gives it when by the word of the gospel he offers it for us to partake, inasmuch as it was crucified, when he seals such giving of himself by the sacred mystery of the Supper, and when he inwardly fulfills what he outwardly designates.

Now here we ought to guard against two faults. First, we should not, by too little regard for the signs, divorce them from their mysteries, to which they are so to speak attached. Secondly, we should not, by extolling them immoderately, seem to obscure somewhat the mysteries themselves.

IV.xvii.11 I therefore say (what has always been accepted in the church and is today taught by all of sound opinion) that the sacred mystery of the Supper consists in two things:

physical signs, which, thrust before our eyes, represent to us, according to our feeble capacity, things invisible; and spiritual truth, which is at the same time represented and displayed through the symbols themselves.

When I wish to show the nature of this truth in familiar terms, I usually set down three things: the signification, the matter that depends upon it, and the power or effect that follows from both. The signification is contained in the promises, which are, so to speak, implicit in the sign. I call Christ with his death and resurrection the matter, or substance. But by effect I understand redemption, righteousness, sanctification, and eternal life, and all the other benefits Christ gives to us. . . .

I say, therefore, that in the mystery of the Supper, Christ is truly shown to us through the symbols of bread and wine, his very body and blood, in which he has fulfilled all obedience to obtain righteousness for us. Why? First, that we may grow into one body with him; secondly, having been made partakers of his substance, that we may also feel his power in partaking of all his benefits.

IV.xvii.19 We must establish such a presence of Christ in the Supper as may neither fasten him to the element of bread, nor enclose him in bread, nor circumscribe him in any way (all which things, it is clear, detract from his heavenly glory); finally, such as may not take from him his own stature, or parcel him out to many places at once, or invest him with boundless magnitude to be spread through heaven and earth. For these things are plainly in conflict with a nature truly human. Let us never (I say) allow these two limitations to be taken away from us: (1) Let nothing be withdrawn from Christ's heavenly glory—as happens when he is brought under the corruptible elements of this world, or bound to any earthly creatures. (2) Let nothing inappropriate to human nature be ascribed to his body, as happens when it is said either to be infinite or to be put in a number of places at once.

IV.xvii.20 Three Evangelists and Paul relate that Christ took the bread, and giving thanks broke it, gave it to his disciples, and said: [Matt. 26:26 (cf. Mark 14:22; 1 Cor. 11:24)]: "Take, eat; this is my body" [ibid., Vg.] "which is given [or broken] for you" [1 Cor. 11:24, Vg.]. Of the cup, Matthew and Mark speak as follows: "This cup is the blood of the New Testament, which is shed for many for forgiveness of sins" [Matt. 26:28; cf. Mark 14:24]. But Paul and Luke say, "This cup is the

New Testament in my blood" [1 Cor. 11:25, Vg.; cf. Luke 22:20].

The defenders of transubstantiation would have the pronoun "this" refer to form of bread, because the consecration is effected by the whole content of the utterance, and there is no substance that can be pointed to. . . .

Those who speak more moderately, although they insist upon the letter, "This is my body," still afterward abandon their rigor and say that it amounts to the same thing as that the body of Christ is with the bread, in the bread, and under the bread.

IV.xvii.31   Greatly mistaken are those who conceive no presence of flesh in the Supper unless it lies in the bread. For thus they leave nothing to the secret working of the Spirit, which unites Christ himself to us. To them Christ does not seem present unless he comes down to us. As though, if he should lift us to himself, we should not just as much enjoy his presence! The question is therefore only of the manner, for they place Christ in the bread, while we do not think it lawful for us to drag him from heaven. Let our readers decide which one is more correct. Only away with that calumny that Christ is removed from his Supper unless he lies hidden under the covering of bread! For since this mystery is heavenly, there is no need to draw Christ to earth that he may be joined to us.

IV.xvii.32   Now, if anyone should ask me how this takes place, I shall not be ashamed to confess that it is a secret too lofty for either my mind to comprehend or my words to declare. And, to speak more plainly, I rather experience than understand it. Therefore, I here embrace without controversy the truth of God in which I may safely rest. He declares his flesh the food of my soul, his blood its drink [John 6:53 ff.]. I offer my soul to him to be fed with such food. In his Sacred Supper he bids me take, eat, and drink his body and blood under the symbols of bread and wine. I do not doubt that he himself truly presents them, and that I receive them. . . . Such is the presence of the body (I say) that the nature of the Sacrament requires a presence which we say manifests itself here with a power and effectiveness so great that it not only brings an undoubted assurance of eternal life to our minds, but also assures us of the immortality of our flesh. Indeed, it is now quickened by his immortal flesh, and in a sense partakes of his immortality.

IV.xvii.43 As for the outward ceremony of the action—whether or not the believers take it in their hands, or divide it among themselves, or severally eat what has been given to each; whether they hand the cup back to the deacon or give it to the next person; whether the bread is leavened or unleavened; the wine red or white—it makes no difference. These things are indifferent, and left at the church's discretion. . . .

The Supper could have been administered most becomingly if it were set before the church very often, and at least once a week. First, then, it should begin with public prayers. After this a sermon should be given. Then, when bread and wine have been placed on the Table, the minister should repeat the words of institution of the Supper. Next, he should recite the promises which were left to us in it; at the same time, he should excommunicate all who are debarred from it by the Lord's prohibition. Afterward, he should pray that the Lord, with the kindness wherewith he has bestowed this sacred food upon us, also teach and form us to receive it with faith and thankfulness of heart, and, inasmuch as we are not so of ourselves, by his mercy make us worthy of such a feast. But here either psalms should be sung, or something be read, and in becoming order the believers should partake of the most holy banquet, the ministers breaking the bread and giving the cup. When the Supper is finished, there should be an exhortation to sincere faith and confession of faith, to love and behavior worthy of Christians. At the last, thanks should be given, and praises sung to God. When these things are ended, the church should be dismissed in peace.

IV.xviii.19 My readers now possess, collected into summary form, almost everything that I thought should be known concerning these two sacraments, whose use has been handed down to the Christian church from the beginning of the New Testament even to the end of the world; that is, that baptism should be, as it were, an entry into the church, and an initiation into faith; but the Supper should be a sort of continual food on which Christ spiritually feeds the household of his believers. Therefore, as there is but one God, one faith, one Christ, and one church, his body; so baptism is but one [Eph. 4:4–6], and is not a thing oft-repeated. But the Supper is repeatedly distributed, that those who have once been drawn into the church may realize that they continually feed upon Christ.

Apart from these two, no other sacrament has been instituted by God, so the church of believers ought to recognize no other; for erecting and establishing new sacraments is not a matter of human choice. We shall readily understand this if we remember what was explained plainly enough above: that sacraments have been appointed by God to instruct us concerning some promise of his, and to attest to us his good will toward us. Moreover, we shall realize this if we bear in mind that no man has been God's counselor [Isa. 40:13; Rom. 11:34], that he should be able to promise anything certain concerning God's will, or assure us and make us confident of what attitude he bears toward us, what he intends to give and what to deny us. At once it is indicated that no man can set forth a sign to be a testimony of any intention or promise of His. It is He alone who has given the sign and can bear witness of himself among us. I will say it more briefly and perhaps more rudely, but more plainly: there can never be a sacrament without promise of salvation. All men assembled together can promise us nothing concerning our salvation. Therefore, they cannot of themselves produce and set up a sacrament.

XXV

THE CHURCH AND THE STATE

1. SPIRITUAL AND CIVIL GOVERNMENT

IV.xx.1   Since we have established above that man is under a twofold government, and since we have elsewhere discussed at sufficient length the kind that resides in the soul or inner man and pertains to eternal life, this is the place to say something also about the other kind, which pertains only to the establishment of civil justice and outward morality.

For although this topic seems by nature alien to the spiritual doctrine of faith which I have undertaken to discuss, what follows will show that I am right in joining them, in fact, that necessity compels me to do so. This is especially true since, from one side, insane and barbarous men furiously strive to overturn this divinely established order; while, on the other side, the flatterers of princes, immoderately praising their power, do not hesitate to set them against the rule of God himself. Unless both these evils are checked, purity of faith will perish. . . .

For certain men, when they hear that the gospel promises a freedom that acknowledges no king and no magistrate among men, but looks to Christ alone, think that they cannot benefit by their freedom so long as they see any power set up over them. They therefore think that nothing will be safe unless the whole world is reshaped to a new form, where there are neither courts, nor laws, nor magistrates, nor anything which in their opinion restricts their freedom. But whoever knows how to distinguish between body and soul, between this present fleeting life and that future eternal life, will without difficulty know that Christ's spiritual Kingdom and the civil jurisdiction are things completely distinct.

IV.xx.2   Yet this distinction does not lead us to consider the
              whole nature of government a thing polluted, which
has nothing to do with Christian men. That is what, indeed,
certain fanatics who delight in unbridled license shout and
boast: after we have died through Christ to the elements of this
world [Col. 2:20], are transported to God's Kingdom, and sit
among heavenly beings, it is a thing unworthy of us and set far
beneath our excellence to be occupied with those vile and
worldly cares which have to do with business foreign to a
Christian man. To what purpose, they ask, are there laws without trials and tribunals? But what has a Christian man to do
with trials themselves? Indeed, if it is not lawful to kill, why do
we have laws and trials? But as we have just now pointed out
that this kind of government is distinct from that spiritual and
inward Kingdom of Christ, so we must know that they are not
at variance. For spiritual government, indeed, is already ini-
tiating in us upon earth certain beginnings of the Heavenly
Kingdom, and in this mortal and fleeting life affords a certain
forecast of an immortal and incorruptible blessedness. Yet civil
government has as its appointed end, so long as we live among
men, to cherish and protect the outward worship of God, to
defend sound doctrine of piety and the position of the church,
to adjust our life to the society of men, to form our social
behavior to civil righteousness, to reconcile us with one another, and to promote general peace and tranquillity. All of
this I admit to be superfluous, if God's Kingdom, such as it is
now among us, wipes out the present life. But if it is God's will
that we go as pilgrims upon the earth while we aspire to the
true fatherland, and if the pilgrimage requires such helps,
those who take these from man deprive him of his very humanity. Our adversaries claim that there ought to be such great
perfection in the church of God that its government should
suffice for law. But they stupidly imagine such a perfection as
can never be found in a community of men. For since the
insolence of evil men is so great, their wickedness so stubborn,
that it can scarcely be restrained by extremely severe laws,
what do we expect them to do?

IV.xx.3   [The function of civil government] among men is no
              less than that of bread, water, sun, and air; indeed, its
place of honor is far more excellent. For it does not merely see
to it, as all these serve to do, that men breathe, eat, drink, and
are kept warm, even though it surely embraces all these activi-
ties when it provides for their living together. It does not, I

repeat, look to this only, but also prevents idolatry, sacrilege against God's name, blasphemies against his truth, and other public offenses against religion from arising and spreading among the people; it prevents the public peace from being disturbed; it provides that each man may keep his property safe and sound; that men may carry on blameless intercourse among themselves; that honesty and modesty may be preserved among men. In short, it provides that a public manifestation of religion may exist among Christians, and that humanity be maintained among men.

Let no man be disturbed that I now commit to civil government the duty of rightly establishing religion, which I seem above to have put outside of human decision. For, when I approve of a civil administration that aims to prevent the true religion which is contained in God's law from being openly and with public sacrilege violated and defiled with impunity, I do not here, any more than before, allow men to make laws according to their own decision concerning religion and the worship of God.

But my readers, assisted by the very clarity of the arrangement, will better understand what is to be thought of the whole subject of civil government if we discuss its parts separately. These are three: the magistrate, who is the protector and guardian of the laws; the laws, according to which he governs; the people, who are governed by the laws and obey the magistrate.

Let us, then, first look at the office of the magistrate, noting whether it is a lawful calling approved of God; the nature of the office; the extent of its power; then, with what laws a Christian government ought to be governed; and finally, how the laws benefit the people, and what obedience is owed to the magistrate.

2. THE FUNCTION AND AUTHORITY OF CIVIL RULERS

IV.xx.4   The Lord has not only testified that the office of magistrate is approved by and acceptable to him, but he also sets out its dignity with the most honorable titles and marvelously commends it to us. . . . Accordingly, no one ought to doubt that civil authority is a calling, not only holy and lawful before God, but also the most sacred and by far the most honorable of all callings in the whole life of mortal men.

IV.xx.6   This consideration ought continually to occupy the magistrates themselves, since it can greatly spur them to exercise their office and bring them remarkable comfort to mitigate the difficulties of their task, which are indeed many and burdensome. For what great zeal for uprightness, for prudence, gentleness, self-control, and for innocence ought to be required of themselves by those who know that they have been ordained ministers of divine justice? How will they have the brazenness to admit injustice to their judgment seat, which they are told is the throne of the living God? How will they have the boldness to pronounce an unjust sentence, by that mouth which they know has been appointed an instrument of divine truth? With what conscience will they sign wicked decrees by that hand which they know has been appointed to record the acts of God? To sum up, if they remember that they are vicars of God, they should watch with all care, earnestness, and diligence, to represent in themselves to men some image of divine providence, protection, goodness, benevolence, and justice. . . . If they commit some fault, they are not only wrongdoers to men whom they wickedly trouble, but are also insulting toward God himself, whose most holy judgments they defile [cf. Isa. 3:14–15].

IV.xx.8   Obviously, it would be an idle pastime for men in private life, who are disqualified from deliberating on the organization of any commonwealth, to dispute over what would be the best kind of government in that place where they live. Also this question admits of no simple solution but requires deliberation, since the nature of the discussion depends largely upon the circumstances. And if you compare the forms of government among themselves apart from the circumstances, it is not easy to distinguish which one of them excels in usefulness, for they contend on such equal terms. The fall from kingdom to tyranny is easy; but it is not much more difficult to fall from the rule of the best men to the faction of a few; yet it is easiest of all to fall from popular rule to sedition. For if the three forms of government which the philosophers discuss be considered in themselves, I will not deny that aristocracy, or a system compounded of aristocracy and democracy, far excels all others: not indeed of itself, but because it is very rare for kings so to control themselves that their will never disagrees with what is just and right; or for them to have been endowed with such great keenness and prudence, that each knows how much is enough. Therefore, men's fault or failing causes it to be safer and more bearable for a number to exercise government, so that they may help one another, teach and admonish one another; and, if one asserts himself unfairly, there may be a number of censors and masters to restrain his willfulness. . . .

I freely admit that no kind of government is more happy than one where freedom is regulated with becoming moderation and is properly established on a durable basis, so also I reckon most happy those permitted to enjoy this state; and if they stoutly and constantly labor to preserve and retain it, I grant that they are doing nothing alien to this office. Indeed, the magistrates ought to apply themselves with the highest diligence to prevent the freedom (whose guardians they have been appointed) from being in any respect diminished, far less be violated. If they are not sufficiently alert and careful, they are faithless in office, and traitors to their country.

But if those to whom the Lord has appointed another form of government should transfer this very function to themselves, being moved to desire a change of government—even to think of such a move will not only be foolish and superfluous, but altogether harmful. However, as you will surely find if you fix your eyes not on one city alone, but look around and glance at the world as a whole, or at least cast your sight upon regions farther off, divine providence has wisely arranged that various countries should be ruled by various kinds of government. For as elements cohere only in unequal proportion, so countries are best held together according to their own particular inequality.

IV.xx.9   We ought to explain in passing the office of the magistrates, how it is described in the Word of God and the things in which it consists. If Scripture did not teach that it extends to both Tables of the Law, we could learn this from secular writers: for no one has discussed the office of magistrates, the making of laws, and public welfare, without beginning at religion and divine worship. And thus all have confessed that no government can be happily established unless piety is the first concern; and that those laws are preposterous which neglect God's right and provide only for men. . . .

As far as the Second Table is concerned, Jeremiah admonishes kings to "do justice and righteousness," to "deliver him who has been oppressed by force from the hand of the oppressor," not to "grieve or wrong the alien, the widow, and the fatherless" or "shed innocent blood" [Jer. 22:3; cf. Vg.]. . . . We see, therefore, that they are ordained protectors and vindicators of public innocence, modesty, decency, and tranquillity, and that their sole endeavor should be to provide for the common safety and peace of all. . . . Justice, indeed, is to receive into safekeeping, to embrace, to protect, vindicate, and free the innocent. But judgment is to withstand the boldness of the impious, to repress their violence, to punish their misdeeds.

IV.xx.10   But here a seemingly hard and difficult question arises: if the law of God forbids all Christians to kill [Ex. 20:13; Deut. 5:17; Matt. 5:21], and the prophet prophesies concerning God's holy mountain (the church) that in it men shall not afflict or hurt [Isa. 11:9; 65:25]—how can magistrates be pious men and shedders of blood at the same time? Yet if we understand that the magistrate in administering punishments does nothing by himself, but carries out the very judgments of God, we shall not be hampered by this scruple. . . . Yet it is necessary for the magistrate to pay attention . . . lest by excessive severity he either harm more than heal; or, by superstitious affectation of clemency, fall into the cruelest gentleness, if he should (with a soft and dissolute kindness) abandon many to their destruction. . . . It is indeed bad to live under a prince with whom nothing is permitted; but much worse under one by whom everything is allowed.

IV.xx.11   Kings and people must sometimes take up arms to execute such public vengeance. On this basis we may judge wars lawful which are so undertaken. For if power has been given them to preserve the tranquillity of their dominion, to restrain the seditious stirrings of restless men, to help those forcibly oppressed, to punish evil deeds—can they use it more opportunely than to check the fury of one who disturbs both the repose of private individuals and the common tranquillity of all, who raises seditious tumults, and by whom violent oppressions and vile misdeeds are perpetrated? If they ought to be the guardians and defenders of the laws, they should also overthrow the efforts of all whose offenses corrupt the discipline of the laws. Indeed, if they rightly punish those robbers whose harmful acts have affected only a few, will they allow a whole country to be afflicted and devastated by robberies with impunity? For it makes no difference whether it be a king or the lowest of the common folk who invades a foreign country in which he has no right, and harries it as an enemy. All such must, equally, be considered as robbers and punished accordingly. Therefore, both natural equity and the nature of the office dictate that princes must be armed not only to restrain the misdeeds of private individuals by judicial punishment, but also to defend by war the dominions entrusted to their safekeeping, if at any time they are under enemy attack. And the Holy Spirit declares such wars to be lawful by many testimonies of Scripture.

IV.xx.12   If anyone object against me that in the New Testament there exists no testimony or example which teaches that war is a thing lawful for Christians, I answer first that the reason for waging war which existed of old still persists today; and that, on the other hand, there is no reason that bars magistrates from defending their subjects. Secondly, I say that an express declaration of this matter is not to be sought in the writings of the apostles; for their purpose is not to fashion a civil government, but to establish the spiritual Kingdom of Christ. Finally, that it is there shown in passing that Christ by his coming has changed nothing in this respect. . . .

But it is the duty of all magistrates here to guard particularly against giving vent to their passions even in the slightest degree. Rather, if they have to punish, let them not be carried away with headlong anger, or be seized with hatred, or burn with implacable severity. Let them also (as Augustine says) have pity on the common nature in the one whose special fault they are punishing. Or, if they must arm themselves against the enemy, that is, the armed robber, let them not lightly seek occasion to do so; indeed, let them not accept the occasion when offered, unless they are driven to it by extreme necessity. For if we must perform much more than the heathen philosopher required when he wanted war to seem a seeking of peace, surely everything else ought to be tried before recourse is had to arms. . . .

Moreover, this same right to wage war furnishes the reason for garrisons, leagues, and other civil defenses. Now, I call "garrisons," those troops which are stationed among the cities to defend the boundaries of a country; "leagues," those pacts which are made by neighboring princes to the end that if any trouble should happen in their lands, they may come to one another's aid, and join forces to put down the common enemies of mankind. I call "civil defenses," things used in the art of war.

IV.xx.13   Lastly, I also wish to add this, that tributes and taxes are the lawful revenues of princes, which they may chiefly use to meet the public expenses of their office; yet they may similarly use them for the magnificence of their household, which is joined, so to speak, with the dignity of the authority they exercise. . . . Princes themselves will in turn remember that their revenues are not so much their private chests as the treasuries of the entire people (for Paul so testifies [Rom. 13:6]), which cannot be squandered or despoiled without manifest injustice. Or rather, that these are almost the very blood of the people, which it would be the harshest inhumanity not to spare. Moreover, let them consider that their imposts and levies, and other kinds of tributes are nothing but supports of public necessity; but that to impose them upon the common folk without cause is tyrannical extortion. These considerations do not encourage princes to waste and expensive luxury, as there is surely no need to add fuel to their cupidity, already too much kindled of itself.

3. THE NATURE OF CIVIL LAWS

IV.xx.14   Next to the magistracy in the civil state come the laws, stoutest sinews of the commonwealth, or, as Cicero, after Plato, calls them, the souls, without which the magistracy cannot stand, even as they themselves have no force apart from the magistracy. Accordingly, nothing truer could be said than that the law is a silent magistrate; the magistrate, a living law.

IV.xx.15   Every nation is left free to make such laws as it foresees to be profitable for itself. Yet these must be in conformity to that perpetual rule of love, so that they indeed vary in form but have the same purpose.

IV.xx.16   The statement of some, that the law of God given through Moses is dishonored when it is abrogated and new laws preferred to it, is utterly vain. For others are not preferred to it when they are more approved, not by a simple comparison, but with regard to the condition of times, place, and nation; or when that law is abrogated which was never enacted for us. For the Lord through the hand of Moses did not give that law to be proclaimed among all nations and to be in force everywhere; but when he had taken the Jewish nation into his safekeeping, defense, and protection, he also willed to be a lawgiver especially to it; and—as became a wise lawgiver—he had special concern for it in making its laws.

4. THE CHRISTIAN ATTITUDE
TOWARD THE STATE

IV.xx.17   It now remains for us to examine . . . what usefulness
the laws, judgments, and magistrates have for the
common society of Christians. To this is also joined another
question: how much deference private individuals ought to
yield to their magistrates, and how far their obedience ought
to go.

IV.xx.18   Lawsuits are permissible if rightly used. There is right
use, both for the plaintiff in suing and for the accused
in defending himself, if the defendant presents himself on the
appointed day and with such exception, as he can, defends
himself without bitterness, but only with this intent, to defend
what is his by right, and if on the other hand, the plaintiff,
undeservedly oppressed either in his person or in his property,
puts himself in the care of the magistrate, makes his complaint,
and seeks what is fair and good. But he should be far from all
passion to harm or take revenge, far from harshness and hatred, far from burning desire for contention. He should rather
be prepared to yield his own and suffer anything than be carried away with enmity toward his adversary. On the other
hand, where hearts are filled with malice, corrupted by envy,
inflamed with wrath, breathing revenge, finally so inflamed
with desire for contention, that love is somewhat impaired in
them, the whole court action of even the most just cause cannot but be impious. For this must be a set principle for all
Christians: that a lawsuit, however just, can never be rightly
prosecuted by any man, unless he treat his adversary with
the same love and good will as if the business under controversy were already amicably settled and composed. Perhaps
someone will interpose here that such moderation is so uni-
formly absent from any lawsuit that it would be a miracle if
any such were found. Indeed, I admit that, as the customs of
these times go, an example of an upright litigant is rare; but the
thing itself, when not corrupted by the addition of anything
evil, does not cease to be good and pure. But when we hear
that the help of the magistrate is a holy gift of God, we must
more diligently guard against its becoming polluted by our
fault.

IV.xx.22   The first duty of subjects toward their magistrates is
to think most honorably of their office, which they
recognize as a jurisdiction bestowed by God, and on that ac-

count to esteem and reverence them as ministers and representatives of God. . . .

I am not discussing the men themselves, as if a mask of dignity covered foolishness, or sloth, or cruelty, as well as wicked morals full of infamous deeds, and thus acquired for vices the praise of virtues; but I say that the order itself is worthy of such honor and reverence that those who are rulers are esteemed among us, and receive reverence out of respect for their lordship.

IV.xx.23   From this also something else follows: that, with hearts inclined to reverence their rulers, the subjects should prove their obedience toward them, whether by obeying their proclamations, or by paying taxes, or by undertaking public offices and burdens which pertain to the common defense, or by executing any other commands of theirs. . . .

Under this obedience I include the restraint which private citizens ought to bid themselves keep in public, that they may not deliberately intrude in public affairs, or pointlessly invade the magistrate's office, or undertake anything at all politically. If anything in a public ordinance requires amendment, let them not raise a tumult, or put their hands to the task—all of them ought to keep their hands bound in this respect—but let them commit the matter to the judgment of the magistrate, whose hand alone here is free. I mean, let them not venture on anything without a command. For when the ruler gives his command, private citizens receive public authority.

IV.xx.24   Since we have so far been describing a magistrate who truly is what he is called, that is, a father of his country, and, as the poet expresses it, shepherd of his people, guardian of peace, protector of righteousness, and avenger of innocence—he who does not approve of such government must rightly be regarded as insane.

But it is the example of nearly all ages that some princes are careless about all those things to which they ought to have given heed, and, far from all care, lazily take their pleasure. Others, intent upon their own business, put up for sale laws, privileges, judgments, and letters of favor. Others drain the common people of their money, and afterward lavish it on insane largesse. Still others exercise sheer robbery, plundering houses, raping virgins and matrons, and slaughtering the innocent.

Consequently, many cannot be persuaded that they ought to recognize these as princes and to obey their authority as far as possible. For in such great disgrace, and among such crimes, so alien to the office not only of a magistrate but also of a man, they discern no appearance of the image of God which ought to have shone in the magistrate; while they see no trace of that minister of God, who had been appointed to praise the good, and to punish the evil [cf. 1 Peter 2:14, Vg.]. Thus, they also do not recognize as ruler him whose dignity and authority Scripture commends to us. Indeed, this inborn feeling has always been in the minds of men to hate and curse tyrants as much as to love and venerate lawful kings.

IV.xx.25   But if we look to God's Word, it will lead us farther.

We are not only subject to the authority of princes who perform their office toward us uprightly and faithfully as they ought, but also to the authority of all who, by whatever means, have got control of affairs, even though they perform not a whit of the princes' office. For despite the Lord's testimony that the magistrate's office is the highest gift of his beneficence to preserve the safety of men, and despite his appointment of bounds to the magistrates—he still declares at the same time that whoever they may be, they have their authority solely from him. Indeed, he says that those who rule for the public benefit are true patterns and evidences of this beneficence of his; that they who rule unjustly and incompetently have been raised up by him to punish the wickedness of the people; that all equally have been endowed with that holy majesty with which he has invested lawful power.

IV.xx.29   We owe this attitude of reverence and therefore of piety toward all our rulers in the highest degree, whatever they may be like. I therefore the more often repeat this: that we should learn not to examine the men themselves, but take it as enough that they bear, by the Lord's will, a character upon which he has imprinted and engraved an inviolable majesty.

But (you will say) rulers owe responsibilities in turn to their subjects. This I have already admitted. But if you conclude from this that service ought to be rendered only to just governors, you are reasoning foolishly. For husbands are also bound to their wives, and parents to their children, by mutual responsibilities. Suppose parents and husbands depart from their duty. Suppose parents show themselves so hard and intractable to their children, whom they are forbidden to provoke to anger [Eph. 6:4], that by their rigor they tire them beyond measure. Suppose husbands most despitefully use their wives,

whom they are commanded to love [Eph. 5:25] and to spare
as weaker vessels [1 Peter 3:7]. Shall either children be less
obedient to their parents or wives to their husbands? . . .

If we are greedily despoiled by one who is avaricious or
wanton, if we are neglected by a slothful one, if finally we are
vexed for piety's sake by one who is impious and sacrilegious,
let us first be mindful of our own misdeeds, which without
doubt are chastised by such whips of the Lord [cf. Dan. 9:7].
By this, humility will restrain our impatience. Let us then also
call this thought to mind, that it is not for us to remedy such
evils; that only this remains, to implore the Lord's help, in
whose hand are the hearts of kings, and the changing of king-
doms [Prov. 21:1 p]. "He is God who will stand in the assembly
of the gods, and will judge in the midst of the gods" [Ps.
82:1 p].

IV.xx.30   Here are revealed his goodness, his power, and his
            providence. For sometimes he raises up open aveng-
ers from among his servants, and arms them with his command
to punish the wicked government and deliver his people, oppressed in unjust ways, from miserable calamity. Sometimes he
directs to this end the rage of men with other intentions and
other endeavors.

IV.xx.32   In that obedience which we have shown to be due the
            authority of rulers, we are always to make this excep-
tion, indeed, to observe it as primary, that such obedience is
never to lead us away from obedience to him, to whose will the
desires of all kings ought to be subject, to whose decrees all
their commands ought to yield, to whose majesty their scep-
ters ought to be submitted. And how absurd would it be that
in satisfying men you should incur the displeasure of him for
whose sake you obey men themselves! The Lord, therefore, is
the King of Kings, who, when he has opened his sacred mouth,
must alone be heard, before all and above all men; next to him
we are subject to those men who are in authority over us, but
only in him. If they command anything against him, let it go
unesteemed. And here let us not be concerned about all that
dignity which the magistrates possess; for no harm is done to
it when it is humbled before that singular and truly supreme
power of God.

G O D   B E   P R A I S E D